Smoking Guns and Paper Trails

How Your Words and Actions in the Workplace BACKFIRE

What *you* need to know to protect yourself and your company

Jack Tapper

Simon-William Publishing, Inc.
Memphis, TN

Publisher's Cataloging-in-Publication Data

(Provided by Quality Books, Inc.)

Tapper, Jack.
    Smoking guns and paper trails : how your words and actions in the workplace backfire : what you need to know to protect yourself and your company / Jack Tapper. --1st ed.
    p. cm.
Includes index.

LCCN 2001119598
ISBN 0-9716084-1-5

1. Business records--Management. 2. Information resources management. 3. Management. 4. Executives--United States--Handbooks, manuals, etc. 5. Business law--United States--Popular works. 6. Liability (Law)--United States--Popular works. I. Title.

HF5736.T36 2002   651.5'1

QB133-651

This publication is designed to provide accurate and authoritative information with regard to the subject matter covered. It is sold with the understanding that the publisher is not engaged in rendering legal, accounting, or other professional advice. If legal advice or other expert assistance is required, the services of a competent professional person should be sought."--from a Declaration of Principles jointly adopted by a Committee of the American Bar Association and a Committee of Publishers and Associations.

Published by

Simon-William Publishing, Inc.

P.O. Box 17123, Memphis, TN 38187-0123

Printed in the United States of America
Cover design by George Foster (Foster & Foster, Inc.)

To my best friend and life-long love, my wife Candy,
who kept singing the song in my heart whenever I forgot
the words

Disclaimer

The information in this book is for educational and informational purposes only. It is intended to help you understand particular issues, but is not intended as an exhaustive treatise on any of the subjects. The author's discussions and opinions are not intended to create any attorney-client relationship between the author or the publisher, and the reader. Your purchase of this book does not constitute such a relationship.

You should not act on any advice or opinion contained in any of these chapters without first consulting with your or your company's lawyers. In law, the right solution for any problem or issue depends on the specific facts of each situation, and although you read about other situations or cases that appear similar to your own, you cannot rely on, or expect, a similar outcome in yours. No two cases are exactly alike in all facts and circumstances. The outcome from applying laws to facts can change significantly when just one fact changes, and that fact could be the industry you're working in, a regulation governing your work, a company policy, your geographical location, the court that reviews the issues, the type of product involved, the social context in which a problem arises, the manner in which it arises...and much more. Don't play lawyer with the laws. Consult with your own or your company's counsel for the course of action that's correct for you and your company.

Use the information in this book to make you aware of issues and to sensitize you to the liability potentials of your surroundings.

Acknowledgments

To George Foster, many thanks for your expertise in creating the front and back cover designs. You were a joy to work with.

To Rudy Zak, a friend and inspiration: Your letter to me expressing your support (during a difficult time of endurance in the writing process) will never be forgotten. It humbled me into realizing how sincere you are about "commitment," and believing in dreams. As a retired WWII, U.S. military officer, you're a role model for character, integrity, and independent spirit—a fine and decent man, and one of America's heroes. I shall always remember you, and value your friendship.

And to my brother Steve, thank you for always being there. You're not just a brother, you're also a "best" friend, a trusted confidante, and motivational guru. Although you were busy building houses while I was building a book, your encouragement throughout the project was comforting, and reassuring. You're always inspirational, and a task master for getting things done.

To Candy—my wife, anchor, and mentor, throughout this process: It could not have been done without your tenacity to see it through, and your persistent encouragement to make it happen. Your critiques of early chapters, and creative ideas, added so much value, not to mention your hugs and loving words during many late nights. Your faith and belief in me are exhilarating. Our bond is a blessing.

My daughter trumped through several early chapter drafts, and gave me some bright new approaches to the material, to keep it focused for non-lawyers. Thanks, Lindsey, for your help and encouragement, through e-mails and telephone calls, while away at college. To my son Dean, your positive spirit always came through in our conversations. You helped to keep me visualizing the goal, and I felt your sense of pride the whole time. What I taught you and Lindsey through your childhood years about positive thinking apparently took hold. As adults, you returned to me what I had so steadily preached to you. (To parents everywhere, when you think they're not listening, they really are.) You gave me all the "space" I needed to work on this project, and even learned, after the first thirty times, to stop asking, "Is it done yet?"

Thanks, also, to those who have helped to shape my career in law and teaching through the years. My early role model, and mentor, was The Hon. Martin L. Haines, retired Judge of the Superior Court of New Jersey. I had the honor and privilege of partnering with him in a law firm, before he ascended to the bench. He stands out as the "lawyer's lawyer," a model of scholarship, integrity, ethics, and advocacy—and, with all that, a real gentleman. My transition from outside counsel to in-house corporate counsel was made opportune in 1990 by James E. Butler, who introduced me to the demanding challenges of general counseling at a major hotel-casino entertainment complex in Atlantic City. Thanks, James, for that experience. And to E.O. ("Ed") Robinson, Jr., former Sr. Vice-President and General Counsel of Harrah's Entertainment, Inc., thanks for a great experience at corporate headquarters. I always admired your keen insight about corporate politics, diplomacy, and the art of corporate counseling. You created an atmosphere that gave all of the lawyers the opportunity to grow, professionally, and exercise independent judgment.

Of the many fine and talented outside counsel, with whom I've worked on lawsuits defending our clients in the Fortune 500 world, some, in particular, deserve special recognition, as superb trial lawyers: Russell Lichtenstein, of Cooper Perskie (Atlantic City, NJ), R. David Kaufman, of Brunini, Grantham, Grower & Hewes PLLC (Jackson MS), Stanley Siegel and Patrick Sauter of Rider Bennett Egan & Arundel (Minneapolis, MN), Glenn Ronaldson (Ronaldson & Kuchler, Chicago, IL), Chris Johnston (Querry & Harrow, Chicago, IL), Daniel

Newman (West Orange, NJ), Robert L. Moore, of Thomason Hendrix (Memphis, TN), Art Tuverson, of Tuverson & Hilyard (Los Angeles, CA), and Jerry Marks of Marks O'Neill Reilly O'Brien & Courtney (Philadelphia, PA). We went through a lot in the trenches, with a highly successful and remarkable record. All of those experiences were enriching and enlightening, not only from our side of the battle, but from what we discovered, and dealt with, on the other. The "war" stories seem amusing now, but they weren't at the time. Strategy is (and always will be) the winning element, and you were always at the top of the game. That puts you at the top of my list, where only the best can be.

My success in managing a volume of nationwide cases was also due, in no small part, to the stellar performances of two of my legal assistants, Kathy Hughes and Colleen Goodspeed, who were with me for years as the pulse of our litigation team at Promus Companies and Harrah's. When it comes to the cream of the crop, they're it. And I can't forget the very able contributions of another excellent legal assistant, Mary Kim Shipp, who, in my early corporate days, painstakingly helped to develop our computerized litigation management database, which served us well for many years. As for secretaries, I've never found any finer legal, executive and administrative secretary than Judith L. King, my right arm throughout my early years of private practice in Burlington County, New Jersey. I'm grateful, Judy, for your devotion for twelve of those loyal and memorable years.

Peggy Maitland Henry was my colleague at Burlington County College in Pemberton, New Jersey, who worked so tirelessly on making the Legal Assistant program achieve the standards of approval by the American Bar Association. Peg, you were a model of professionalism, and always so charming, too.

I remember those times in academia with much fondness. And to all my students who suffered through the rigors of my courses, including my weekly quizzes, thank you for allowing me to be part of the shaping of your careers. You humbled, inspired, and enriched me with the experience.

Thanks to all the staff associated with my publisher Simon-William Publishing. You pulled it all together, and made the production from manuscript to book a reality, with smooth efficiency, and professional expertise. Although it all seemed easy, I know it's because of the hard work and dedication your team put into the project.

And in memory of my mom and dad whom I thought about often during the process, I know you're beaming with pride from above.

CONTENTS

Introduction

The world of smoking guns

===

"Gotcha!" That's what a smoking gun says as it discredits you. You say it one way now, but what you said or did before makes it appear otherwise. As a piece of evidence, it doesn't mean you're guilty or at fault, but it provides an enormous advantage for your adversaries, who either use it "as is," or manipulate it, to show you're lying or, at least, not telling the whole story. To your opponent, the advantage of the smoking gun stems from its creator: YOU! It jolts you to the defensive, maligns your integrity, and intimidates your demeanor. If you want to save yourself or your company, though, from that predicament, this book's for you.

The public's familiarity with smoking guns comes mainly from the news media, as they cover stories involving known public figures, and giant companies. What about the internal memo of a top executive at Enron Corp., the utility giant that filed bankruptcy in December, 2001, warning the CEO that the company would "implode in a wave of accounting scandals" if off-the-books partnership deals continued to go unreported? It took center stage as a smoking gun at a U.S. Congressional hearing investigating the activity of Enron officials. How could Enron officials claim not to have known about where the company was headed in the face of such a memo?

Can you remember when the dominant smoking gun in the world's headlines was a DNA specimen on the now infamous navy blue dress worn by Monica Lewinsky? It incriminated a former U.S. President, and forced him to change his public denials of involvement with "that woman."

We've heard and read about smoking gun memos and e-mails written by Microsoft Corp.'s top executives. During the prosecution of an antitrust lawsuit involving Microsoft's *Internet Explorer*, the government used them as a strategy to discredit the executives' denials of anti-competitive intentions. And another well-known company, General Motors, had its share of media attention. It was hit with a staggering verdict of $4.9 billion in a product liability suit in Los Angeles, over an alleged faulty fuel tank design in its Chevy Malibu. The jury was inflamed by a smoking gun over 26 years old—an internal memo from one of GM's engineers. (We'll use this in Chapter 11 as an example of what *not* to write in your company's internal reports.) Then, there's Texaco, the oil giant, which paid $176 million to settle a racial discrimination suit by employees after its smoking guns—tape recordings of senior executives—revealed casual conversations, allegedly filled with racially derogatory remarks.

Although the list goes on and never seems to end, this book could save you and your company from getting a place on it. "Smoking guns" in the workplace are a preventable malady. Neither you, nor the company, need suffer the repercussions from the kinds of words, deeds, or actions that sabotage your career and the company's winning defense posture. By being alert and informed about the areas that breed smoking guns, you can avoid ever creating them. Everyone in the workplace from CEO to frontline is capable of producing them, and the headlines and stories we read about everyday confirm it. With e-mails and voice mails, the Internet, and everything typed on a keyboard stored as an electronic file, the opportunities for employees to say the wrong thing, do the wrong thing, or send an imprudent message to the wrong people are everywhere. And in the scheme of things, it doesn't matter if your company is big or small, public or private.

In the arena of civil litigation (where lawsuits are filed for money damages, not criminal penalties), smoking guns are found in what you write, as well in other things you or your co-workers do. The writings are usually memos, letters, reports, or notes and diaries, and they're stored in file cabinets, drawers, and archived storage boxes for later discovery. You can also find them in the pictures, notes, and other postings on walls and bulletin boards of offices and manufacturing plants. More commonly today, they're in electronic messages, such as e-mails and word-processed documents. When your company fails to respond attentively to customers' complaints or regulatory compliance notices, and when employees don't supervise or oversee a project with the diligence it needs, or when they get lax on security controls to protect access to data, these all cultivate the breeding grounds for smoking guns.

I'm willing to bet you have smoking guns stored right now on hard drives, back-up tapes, floppy disks, and CD-ROMs. One back-up tape can hold the equivalent of 19 million pages of documents. That's astounding when you think of how many of these tapes you can fit into one file drawer. If you were to convert that drawer into paper files, you would have enough bankers' boxes to fill a storage warehouse the size of a football field. Can you imagine how many smoking guns await discovery in such a drawer?

My mission is to be your straight-talking guide who will

show you where the smoking guns are hiding, alert you to their dangers, and tell you how to avoid creating them. I'll focus on the traps that make civil lawsuits against you and your company lucrative for plaintiffs' lawyers. When you fall into these traps, and create a smoking gun that puts your company (and maybe your job) on the line, the stakes get alarmingly high.

Our journey will begin with an introduction to some of your co-workers whose behavioral traits foster the breeding of smoking guns. You'll be sure to find some familiar behavior here. Then we'll show you how the ground rules for civil litigation empower trial lawyers to invade your workspace, obtain your files, probe your work habits, and attack your hard drives, laptops, and even your personal home computers. To protect yourself from unwittingly creating documents that can backfire, you need to know how intrusive the discovery process is when the "other side" fires their cannons with a lawsuit. We'll also travel into the e-mail jungle, and show you nine traps that can catch you unaware, just by the way you send, receive, and store e-mails and e-files. Beyond e-mails and e-files, we'll explore much more in the breeding grounds for smoking guns, from your use and handling of cell phones, voicemails, faxes, copy centers, and print stations to how you write reports and personnel evaluations, and how to deal with certain risk management issues, including the kind of access you give to outsiders like janitorial crews. And we don't stop there, because we'll visit your own office area and talk about the dangers lurking in your paper shuffle world, how you handle confidential documents, and the ease and dangers of accessing company secrets on the company's database network.

I'll also review real-life examples of the best and worst of corporate crisis management. Sooner or later your company will face a newsworthy crisis, and if you bungle the media and public relations portion of it, you'll open the floodgates for smoking guns and lawsuits. Chapter 9 will show you what happens "when it all hits the fan." I include a 20-Point Guide for managing your public relations during a major crisis event, and my own pronouncement of Eleven Commandments your spokesperson should follow when dealing with the media. We'll also talk about how and why companies get nailed with huge punitive damage verdicts that are all avoidable. I'll demonstrate, by example, what went wrong in two celebrated cases—one involving the ubiquitous, number one fast-food chain, McDonald's, and its hot cup of coffee, and the other, the car company, General Motors,—where juries "punished" the companies with punitive damage verdicts. You'll discover how your company can avoid making the same mistakes and how you can avoid contributing to them.

You don't have to let trial lawyers take advantage of blunders that you or other employees make. You CAN root out this invidious occurrence which, with little doubt, is firmly rooted in *your* company, too. I'll give you what you need to know to *"Gain the advantage before the other side takes it!"*

Throughout this book, I'll also provide you with personal suggestions or techniques (each named a "Tapper's Tip") to help you avoid becoming prey to the plaintiff-predators who have your company in the cross-hairs of their lawsuit scopes. They're reminders for some of the things you need to know. Before long, you'll realize how effectively you can reduce not only your own risk of liability, but the company's, too.

I'm not saying that what you learn here will eliminate lawsuits against your company. Anyone with the power to do that should command far greater than the price of this book. Realistically, in our litigious society where thousands of lawsuits are filed every day, you can't really control who files them, or what they allege you did. But you CAN control which side wins! You have the power to strengthen your defense arsenal—your readiness—for the inevitable attack, and eliminate the handicap of a smoking gun.

To achieve the best results, and the most rewards, for these efforts, your company must become proactive. If, instead, it's in a "wait and see" mode, you'll always be on the defensive, circling your wagons for each onslaught. The plaintiffs and their trial lawyers will come knocking on your doors, serving their lawsuits, and handing you subpoenas for documents that will "smoke 'til you choke." But if you jumpstart your company into a proactive posture, you can, in time, curtail the production of smoking guns so the plaintiffs' trial lawyers come up dry on their search through your records—not because you're hiding anything, but simply because you're smarter, and wiser, about what you write, how you write it, and what you do and say amongst colleagues. You'll be working from a position of strength which will save those hard-earned revenues from getting sucked down the litigation drain with drawn-out legal battles and hasty, costly settlements, caused by words and actions that backfired.

No cover-ups here

Be cautioned that you don't misinterpret my message. This book is not a how-to book for covering up misdeeds. You don't "clean up" smoking guns with a "cover-up," as you'll only create newer, and more devastating ones than those you try to eradicate or obscure. These pages will show you what you need to know to protect yourself and your company from creating smoking guns, and how to keep your words and actions from backfiring. If you heed the wake-up calls, you shouldn't be worried about what you're putting in your files anymore. As to what's already in the company's files (to which you've contributed), there are legal ways and means of purging old documents and messages. The most common is by initiating and enforcing a "document retention" program (where you clean out old documents, according to a detailed and formal timetable that identifies categories of information and tells you how long to hold on to documents, as well as when to discard them). This program is usually integrated with E-mail and Internet usage policies your company should also have in place. Chapter 12 will show you how these programs and policies work, and the points they should cover, if you want a strong, aggressive, and legally effective operation. Although the Enron scandal gave "document retention" a bad name when the untimely (and criminal) shredding of documents took place under the guise of the company's retention program, the fact is these programs, when run legitimately, and in good faith, are not only a legally recognized way of keeping up with the overload of paper and electronic messages, but a good business practice.

Plain-talking, straight-shooting—no "legal jargon"

Many of the issues I discuss have origins in complex legal doctrines, but no need to wince; I have simplified them for discussion. This is not a law book; it's a business book, and I have painstakingly kept that in mind, so there's no legal jargon here. I've kept my writing style colloquial because I want this to be between you and me.

This book is intended for all of you in the business world who face the myriad (and often confusing) concoction of laws, rules, regulations and policies that can trip you into a smoking gun without your knowing it—until it's too late. What you'll discover in these pages will put you giant steps ahead of those colleagues who haven't been enlightened by its contents. And if you're a shareholder in any corporation, you can benefit from what you learn here if you use it to assess whether your company is doing what it should to reduce its vulnerabilities, and thereby, protect your investment. After all, smoking guns weaken the company's defenses, and when they're discovered, and it all "hits the fan," you'll be sure to see and feel the financial impact on your investment. So, it's really everybody's business to stay alert. It can no longer just be the business of the officers, directors, and auditors. As a shareholder, you have voting power to elect the directors annually. Cast that vote with your eyes open.

To my lawyer colleagues: this book is not intended for you, although I welcome your indulgence if you're either an outside or inside counsel, on the "defense" side. Perhaps, you'll also see the value of buying a copy for each of your business clients, and suggesting it as "required" reading. It will make your job easier when they understand the issues you face when you find their smoking "gems" during the arduous process of pretrial discovery and document production.

So, let's get started on the journey through the world of smoking guns. It's time to open your eyes, my friend.

Chapter 1

Loose Cannons

Traits that breed smoking guns

Introducing...

- ☐ **The Butt Protector**
- ☐ **The Yellow Padder**
- ☐ **The "Hot Potato" Head**
- ☐ **The Chest Pounder**
- ☐ **The Marketeer**
- ☐ **The Fire Dragon**

In just about every workplace, certain personality types breed the kinds of words and actions that turn into smoking guns. The people with these traits are loose cannons in your daily operations. I'll introduce you to them by describing their typical behaviors. Once sensitized to their ways, you can avoid getting stuck in the traps they create. This isn't to say they intentionally do this (at least the good-willed ones don't); they usually just don't realize the consequences of what they do (or then again, maybe they do, in which case you need not be a fool to their game).

I'm asking for a bit of indulgence here because my observations aren't based on scientific studies. They're from the laboratory of common sense and sensibility. I don't claim any expertise in psychology, just experience and observations from thirty years in company environments where I have encountered, confronted, and dealt with these loose cannons. By the way, no trait favors any gender, so don't take solace if you're an opposite gender from the loose cannon I describe. Gender designation in this context is a matter of convenience, not substance.

Work environment and stress seem to play a role in fostering these behaviors. When the top dog today can be dog food tomorrow, the competitive corporate world is an engine that powers insecurity. That forces employees (especially at management levels) to look over their shoulders, most of the time, and wonder who's expendable in the next budget cut. But they can also be driven simply by personality, including a positive sense of bravado, where a person thinks aggressiveness makes him stand out from the crowd.

Not that anyone you can identify with these traits should be suspect. It's an irony that the characters I describe may be among the company's best performers who exhibit high integrity and dedication to their jobs. The thing is, there's usually something that motivates these mannerisms. The challenge is to identify what it is so you can more effectively address the cause and eliminate its effect.

If it happens that you find *yourself* uncomfortably described by any of the following traits, you may want to reconsider your modus operandi. You, too, could be a potential problem, not only for the company, but for yourself, when your words and actions backfire. And when that happens, it could be your name on the "Who stays? Who goes?" agenda of the next executive session behind closed doors.

Introductions now, please....

THE BUTT PROTECTOR

This one is easy to spot. He writes a memo confirming everything. Maybe you just finished talking to him via phone conference. Or maybe you just came out of a meeting he called. You'll soon receive a memo "confirming" what was said, sometimes in an "I said—You said" format. If there were other participants, you'll see quotes or paraphrases from them, too. Caution: If things were left a bit ambiguous at the meeting on issues important to the Butt Protector, he may attempt to clear the ambiguity by embellishing the facts to conform them more to his slant on things. He'll underscore how someone was opposed to a particular position (usually one that he favored), or how someone only half-heartedly supported it. Look for the tone or phraseology of this memo, which will be subjective and subtle, with a craftiness or slyness showing through. On the surface, the documented comments of the participants, and the delineation of issues raised, will make it appear as if his purpose is 100% accuracy. But it's not.

These types of memos (referred to in many quarters as "C.Y.A." memos because everyone knows they're written to "cover your ass" if things go awry) are found at all levels of management, and more frequently than you'd think, among upper mid-level managers and key management officers. Regardless of rank, though, the Butt Protector wants to impress his boss, making it look like he's "getting things done." The documented quotes help the Butt Protector "lock" the meeting participants in to the views expressed, so if a project goes "south" the C.Y.A.

memo becomes a useful tool for finger-pointing that either deflects blame away from him or insulates his view among respected peers who shared the same opinion.

When he produces an inaccurate summary, he creates a dilemma, and a potential smoking gun, or backfiring memorandum: Should someone on the receiving end respond with a correction, and if so, how? On one hand, to avoid creating smoking guns, you should write less, talk more (such as by telephone or face-to-face, without recordings or anyone taking notes) and reduce your paper or electronic trails. On the other hand, if you don't respond in writing (via paper or e-mail), the content of the Butt Protector's memo remains as a faulty record that could backfire at a much later date (sometimes, years later) when a trial lawyer on the other side wields the memo as proof that what it said happened, actually did. By that time, the inaccuracy has taken root as "the way it was," and very few people, if any, will remember the actual details of what actually happened beyond what's in the original memo as "the record." If a company person who originally attended the meeting or conference that the memo refers to, is still around, and that person tries to discredit the Butt Protector's writing with a "recollection" that contradicts it, the testimony will likely appear disingenuous such a long time after the event. This is particularly so if years have passed and the Butt Protector, no longer with the company, has an employment-related lawsuit pending against the company. Believe it or not, the situation is not that unusual.

Tapper'sTip #1

Writings created contemporaneously with an event tend to have more credibility in the eyes of a jury than someone's "recollection" of the same event several years later. That's why it's so important to timely correct any misquotes or misstatements, while the memo or other writing (through e-mail or any other manner) is still fresh.

Another problem with the C.Y.A. memo is that it tends to reveal too much detail for posterity. We don't need to know all of the off-hand remarks that attendees contributed to a subject, nor do we need a record of their vocalized thought processes that led them to an opinion. The co-workers that "catch on" to the Butt Protector's ways will, over time, clam up in meetings and offer only what they think is satisfactory for quotes on paper. When that happens, you lose the spontaneity of thought and free-spirited exchange of new ideas.

Tapper's Tip #2

Employees who indiscriminately prepare a C.Y.A. memo as a way of recording people's positions should be discouraged from doing so, under threat of termination. Their memo is another paper or electronic record that your company doesn't need in its information archives.

So, what's the best course of action to resolve the dilemma?

■ The Butt Protector's supervisor (or, if the Butt Protector is already a manager, the person to whom he reports) should call him in for a consultation, and get to the core of why he feels the need to write meeting summaries that haven't been requested. Look for hidden issues or reasons beneath his surface response of "protecting the record." Arrange for an appropriate person to address them.

■ If the "record" he created contains inaccuracies, take steps to correct it. Persuade him to send a short, to the point, "clarification." Be sure that all of those on the previous distribution list get a copy of the "clarified" memo.

■ Alternatively, if you are the person inaccurately or unfairly quoted, send a follow-up memo of correction. But do it objectively, not as a personal attack. No need to give a lot of detail to simply correct what was inaccurate. Just refer to the information that "corrects" the misstatement without engaging in a paper battle of words. The exchange can be abruptly ended with something like, "If you don't agree with my recollection, please call me to discuss it." Whatever you do, don't get into a paper or e-mail battle over it. That may create a situation much worse than leaving the inaccuracy uncorrected.

Tapper's Tip #3

When you respond to someone else's memo, use the same method to send it as was used to receive it: e-mail to e-mail or paper-to-paper. When pre-trial discovery takes place and a search turns up a paper memo, for example, filled with inaccuracies, it's more likely that the "response" to it will be found in the same paper file than if the response were in an e-mail on someone's computer mixed with thousands of other e-mails. If you're replying to an e-mail, try to attach the reply to the original e-mail.

E-mail summaries complicate the process. Although you can tell who was copied on the e-mail, will you ever know who was blind-copied? Who downloaded the e-mail by printing it and putting a hard copy in a file? Who "saved" the e-mail message on a hard drive? And, who forwarded that e-mail to somebody else who wasn't on the original list of recipients? Barring the author's cooperation in changing his memo, IF (and that's a big "if") the inaccuracy was substantial, the person affected most by it should send a "corrective" e-mail and copy everyone known to have received the original.

Sometimes, the Butt Protector will tape-record the meeting or telephone conversation. In some jurisdictions, you don't have to be told that the other person is actually taping the conversation for it to be used as evidence, so long as one party to the conversation consents to it—and guess who that might be? You're right...the Butt Protector! It sounds crazy that the law would allow this but it does. So check with your counsel on the law in your jurisdiction. You need to know what your rights are before voicing your opinions at meetings that may be recorded.

Tape recordings have too much potential for misuse. We've all seen how taped comments can be taken out of context and used to provide a distorted view. Just take the sound bites, for example, used in television news when candidates speak during a political campaign, and you'll know how this works. A ten second video/audio blip of a candidate's speech is supposed to give you the essence of what was said in a one-hour talk. And when meetings run too long and boredom sets in (which could be 90% of the time), people get fidgety and start making comments in jest to break up the boredom. They forget that these comments are also being recorded. When played back at a different time, out of the context of the meeting, these comments take on a different meaning--one that might be construed as supporting a racial or sexual discrimination claim. Worse yet, when the recorded comments are transcribed in writing, the written words, without the inflection and tone of the audio, may have a more deleterious effect.

Tapper's Tip #4

Tape recordings should be prohibited as a matter of company policy and allowed only as an exception when there is a compelling reason announced in advance of a meeting. And it should be written as "policy" that the surreptitious tape recording of any individual in the workplace, for any reason, shall result in termination. No excuses. Just, "Goodbye!"

There's a potential drawback to tightening the screws on this loose cannon: Once you forbid transcriptions of meetings through notes or recordings, you might force the Butt Protector to go "underground" by covertly writing up diary notes or memos to himself, or "memos to file" to memorialize meetings or conversations. All of these can accumulate in folders in his file cabinet or on portable disks or on his computer's hard drive. And that spells t-r-o-u-b-l-e.

Tapper's Tip #5

If you don't address the issues that cause the Butt Protector to act as he does, or resolve to end his C.Y.A. writings, be prepared to accept the risk of discovering smoking guns much later, when the plaintiffs' trial lawyers are scaling your walls. Ask yourself, "Will the potential damage be worth it?"

Aside from my disdain for the C.Y.A. memo, there's a strong exception when it comes to the company vs. the employee. Notice that I said in Tapper's Tip #2 this kind of memo should not be used by *employees* "indiscriminately." I did so for a reason: there are times, such as when your company holds a disciplinary meeting with an employee, when it's important for the *company* to protect itself with a C.Y.A. memo. A disgruntled employee, bent on accumulating ammunition for a lawsuit against the company, could have a tendency to stretch the recollection of what company people said during the meeting. For defensive reasons, your company needs an accurate memo that memorializes what was said by each participant. The memo should be timely prepared, almost immediately following the meeting, when the accuracy of what was said is still fresh in everyone's mind.

The difference here from the usual C.Y.A. memo is that the company intentionally sets out to create a mutually agreed upon record for potential use. The memo is presented to the employee promptly after its completion to confirm its accuracy. The company makes changes that may be necessary, so the employee can affirm its accuracy with a signature. Before creating a written record, however, be sure that your company's officials know what to say, and how to say it, to reflect the company's responsibilities under its own policies, and avoid saying the wrong things in view of the complexity of employment laws that come into play.

THE YELLOW PADDER

She comes to the meeting with yellow pad in hand and shows her diligence by taking copious notes. While note-taking is not, in itself, a bad idea, it's what she puts in those notes that causes problems. When other people's comments are committed to writing, it could be troublesome for the people quoted. The Yellow Padder differs from the Butt Protector because she doesn't send her notes to anyone, nor does she turn them into memos. Those notes get filed away, subject to discovery in a lawsuit against your company months, or even years, later. Will you know before it's too late what kind of comments of yours she committed to writing?

Say, for example, that two years later, the Yellow Padder's notes are produced during pre-trial discovery and the plaintiff's lawyer discovers comments in them attributed to you, and you had no idea that any of your prior statements were archived in her writing. Now, picture yourself in a deposition where the plaintiff's lawyer asks you questions based on those comments, and you insist the quotes were inaccurate. He still uses them to throw you off for a smoking gun effect, forcing you into a defensive position, making it seem as if the earlier quotes were the truth, and your present "recollection" is a lie, or, at least, an attempt to backpedal. Yes, my friend, it's a nasty world out there!

Aside from accuracy, the retention period of these notes poses another real problem. How long does she keep them? Does she file them in a project folder? When the project has been completed, is there a procedure to review what is essential for retention and what is not? There's a way to stop accumulating a bunch of notes that no longer have relevance once the project is over: adopt and adhere to a Document Retention Policy. It establishes the holding period for different kinds of information and requires the removal of outdated notes and related materials to eliminate the paper trail (I'll talk about this in Chapter 12).

How do you control the Yellow Padder in a meeting that calls for confidentiality? Before a meeting starts, there should be an announcement on whether the information to be reviewed or revealed is "confidential." Notes should be prohibited if the information is confidential. When they're not prohibited, there should be an understanding of the types of notes considered appropriate. I've attended meetings where the speaker prefaces what he says with, "This is off the record," and the person next to me writes on his notepad, "off record," but continues to jot down what was *not* intended to be recorded in writing, or otherwise.

Tapper's Tip #6

If you're ever speaking "off the record," be sure that everyone in the room has pens down and recorders turned off, and don't hesitate to single out the violators.

THE "HOT POTATO" HEAD

This person tosses a problem to somebody else when he thinks the solution to it won't be favorable, in the corporate political sense. It's a "hot potato" and his objective is to disassociate from it as soon as possible. How does he accomplish the toss? He declares, in his own way, "It's not my job!"

But look out! In passing it off to you, he dramatizes the problem and exaggerates the consequences if you don't accept it as your responsibility to follow through. He makes it appear to be a problem clearly within your job description or function. Exaggerating the issues, he hopes to intimidate you by emphasizing the "urgency" of the situation and making you feel guilty for "dropping the ball," should you turn it down. His only mission: Get rid of it before it explodes on his time clock.

The memo this person writes is a dangerous smoking gun because it will contain phrases that are particularly alarming. Here's a sample sentence from a marketing division employee to an information technology programmer in the I.T. department: "If you don't debug our software immediately to fix this problem, we'll be paying million dollar damages to customers whose credit information gets downloaded by hackers...." Aside from the exaggeration, the memo is based on erroneous assumptions. The "problem," it turns out, has nothing to do with software. On further investigation, which he didn't take the time to pursue beforehand, the customers' credit information was encrypted, fully protected, and of no use in an encrypted form even if it were "hacked" by criminal entry. The real "problem" in this case was actually a simple piece of third-party hardware that didn't function as it should have, and was easily replaced.

Consider, however, a later lawsuit by a customer who alleges that someone stole her identity and misused her credit cards. She sues your company and claims that it's responsible for her situation because of negligent handling of her personal credit information. During pre-trial discovery, the plaintiff's lawyer discovers the Hot Potato Head's memo and puts company managers on the defensive about the "problem" in the software. Your company now has to spend time defending itself against the erroneous and inflammatory statement made by your own employee even though no hackers ever infiltrated your database.

The way to deal with this loose cannon is to disallow any delegation of issues or problems to other co-workers unless a supervisor authorizes it. And if this cannon is a supervisor or manager, the next supervisor up the chain should have the responsibility to approve or disapprove the toss. If the toss is authorized, the reason and urgency for it should be discussed in either a telephone conference or a personal meeting with the colleague who accepts the toss, not in a memo or e-mail that describes a "problem" or its potentially dire consequences.

Tapper's Tip #7

Avoid inflammatory and exaggerated memos that attempt to force and intimidate your colleagues into accepting responsibility to solve a problem. If problem-solving is within the colleague's functional responsibility, there should be no need to spur him into action with a memo that screams like a police siren.

THE CHEST POUNDER

This person, in the immortal words of comedian Rodney Dangerfield, just "gets no respect." "Nobody listens to me" is his refrain. He's not shy about voicing his opinions to his closer colleagues, but his views are not looked upon with much weight by the upper echelon. Sometimes, his status on the management totem pole is not quite respected enough to turn heads. So, he writes his special style of memo with the gusto of a gorilla pounding his chest to show the need to be reckoned with. He's also the person on the sidelines who smiles with an "I told you so" whenever he can.

He, too, will issue the "five-alarm" memo to whoever he thinks will have some interest in the subject, and announce a "serious" problem that, if not corrected, will cause untoward consequences. (He's very much like the Hot Potato Head in that regard, only he's not trying to toss it off; he wants attention for his view.) If, for example, he's the company claims investigator who completes a customer incident report about a lady who allegedly tripped on a torn carpet, he'll write comments, such as, "I told Facilities to fix this carpet several weeks ago, or somebody would get killed tripping over it."

One way or another, this person will exaggerate the issue, get the facts wrong, and act without checking out the details.

If unchecked, this loose cannon will be the renegade employee whose testimony will support the new lawsuit against the company. He'll give a scathing deposition and bring out the memos he saved to prove he "knew" what he was talking about. He's in his glory as the center of attention when the litigation turns on his testimony. As a way to defuse the impact of his writings, the usual company response accuses him of ill-will and ulterior motives, or labels him as a "disgruntled" employee. But that tactic tends to backfire, as jurors can sense a company that's embarrassed by its own employee.

If, however, the problem raised by the employee is an accusation or concern that the company is violating laws or regulations, you cannot dismiss the issue as an exaggeration. When you have a whistleblower, you'd better confront the issue raised and address it with appropriate concern. The personal and financial repercussions of dismissing the issue or treating the whistleblower with disdain can be devastating. That will simply elevate the whistleblower to star status if, and when, it all "hits the fan" in a future public news event.

Witness the internal memo of a top executive officer of Enron Corp., the Houston, Texas-based worldwide utility com-

pany, that warned of impending financial disaster if questionable accounting practices on public financial statements were
not corrected. It wasn't long thereafter that the accounting practices publicly surfaced, forcing the company's stock price to fall
to penny value, and prompting the filing of what was then the
largest bankruptcy case in U.S. history. I'm not suggesting that
the officer's smoking gun memo in this case caused all of the
consequences. It didn't. But it created a situation that should
not have been ignored.

> *Some suggestions to counter the traits of this
> loose cannon:*

√ Train officers and other upper management to end the
inflammatory-style of writing by teaching them the language,
style, and tone that should be used to bring problems and issues
to light.

√ Open a communication line for any employee who
notices or perceives a problem that could put the company at
risk. Make sure that line goes to a responsible person whose
function is to be accountable for follow-through on an employee's
concerns. After reviewing the "problem" with appropriate
people, communicate the results to the employee. Be sure, as a
company, to deal with the issues raised. Don't retaliate against
the employee. Keep the issue as the focus, not the employee. If
you ignore the issue, you'll come to regret it later, as you'll only
be adding to the employee's frustration, forcing him to resolve
the dilemma by blowing the whistle with a devastating smoking
gun memo. Keeping employees informed about issues important
to them makes them realize you're not ignoring their needs
which, in turn, tempers the need to "chest-pound."

√ Encourage employees not to write memos or e-mails

about certain types of issues, but to discuss concerns verbally with supervisors. If you're a supervisor, be accessible because when you're not, memo writing is the favored form of expression.

√ Be sincere in letting employees know their opinions are valued. Show them the company has a forum for discussion and airing of grievances, operational issues, and issues involving risk management. Just be sure that your actions back up your words. Don't promise results if you can't deliver.

Tapper's Tip #8

Accountability requires responsibility, not delegation or excuses. Better to deal with problems brought to light from within than to wait for a lawsuit from without. The more a company listens and resolves operational concerns of its employees, the less need for those employees to vent the problem in a widely distributed memo designed to get attention.

THE MARKETEER

If your company is growth-oriented and somewhat aggressive in its marketing or development plans, you're sure to have a Marketeer in your ranks. She'll use phrases like, "We'll smash the competition," or, "We'll corner the market." Good stuff, you might say. It rouses the troops. But these morale-boosting exhortations will come back to haunt you. When the CEO is on the witness stand in an antitrust lawsuit trying to defend the company's marketing practices as fair and reasonable, this language won't sit well with a jury that has to decide if the company's practices were predatory.

You can find The Marketeer's writing in the company's

strategic planning proposals, advertising campaign collateral, or capital approval requests for a new development project or acquisition. The Marketeer will use sales hype to entice and excite enthusiasm. Beware of the overzealous statement of benefits for a project because if it's part of publicly-disseminated material, you run the risk of a claim for misrepresentation.

Also, look out for the hype in a proposal for new capital that talks about gaining shares of a particular "market." The Marketeer could be boxing your company in to a narrower definition of a "market" than it really wants, for purposes of keeping free of anti-trust activity. If you define the market too narrowly in your internal documents, those documents are discoverable, and can be used against the company when it tries to defend an anti-trust case accusing the company of monopolizing the "market." Your company usually fares better if it can identify the "market" on a broader basis. That could lessen the impact of your alleged influence.

Sometimes, the Marketeer will use nicknames in internal memos to refer to different types of customers by spending habits. For example, in the casino industry, big gamblers are often referred to as "whales," but when taken out of context of the capital approval committee and into the courtroom, an outsider may consider some of the jargon as derogatory. Don't disparage the dignity of your customers with nicknames in internal documents. The lack of sensitivity of the language used in these internal proposals can come back to haunt. Accept the wording only if you're comfortable having it read to a jury in a public courtroom someday, with the press ready to print quotes in their lead articles.

In those companies that have an in-house law department, it would be a wise practice to have all submissions to the capital approval or strategic planning committees reviewed, in advance, by the law department before they are presented officially. The law department can "clear" the language in advance with an eye toward what a plaintiff's trial lawyer might do with it if it were part of some future pre-trial discovery.

In companies that don't have an in-house law department, outside counsel can do the job. Although it's not practical to send every proposal outside for review, it would be worthwhile to have counsel review a year's worth of such proposals to see if the people writing them have been using imprudent wording. If they have, your company should immediately initiate a training program to teach all of the existing and upcoming Marketeers the kinds of wording that should be prohibited, not only to avoid potential problems with antitrust or trade laws, but to stay clear of violating any other regulatory prohibitions that govern your industry.

Tapper's Tip #9

Keep in mind that all of the proposals sent to special decision-making boards, such as a capital approval committee or a strategic development board, are fully discoverable by the company's adversaries in a lawsuit. That means a jury could get to see and read them somewhere in the future. Don't allow references in these proposals that slur the dignity of customers or make the company look like a cutthroat competitor that's willing to bend the law or walk on its edge.

THE "FIRE DRAGON"

This person is angry. He didn't get his way today because no one liked his ideas. Or, maybe he got put down in front of others at a management meeting and his embarrassment boils within. He'll swallow his anger for only so long. Although he's generally an outwardly calm-looking person, he internalizes the emotion, steaming until he blows his cool, and when he does, he won't wait for "cool-down" before responding. He has to let somebody know he's angry. Your e-mail, memo, or telephone call to him may just be his trigger.

In his mouth-foaming state, he'll say things that will embarrass himself when read in a more relaxed state of mind. Yet, his words are recorded for the long term, in a saved e-mail, or a printout. How many people will receive the e-mail or printed memo? It may travel with lightning speed through the company's distribution channels, and if that happens, there's no control on who downloads and prints it. Was the paper copy of the e-mail filed? If so, by whom? And in how many places? Was the memo forwarded to others?

If the Fire Dragon is a manager complaining with derogatory or demoralizing words to his subordinate, we'll assume there's no widespread distribution of such an e-mail or note, but you can count on the subordinate saving the message for posterity. You'll see it again—when the employee sues the company and the manager for discrimination, harassment, or "hostile environment."

One basic principle you should always follow in your work world is to never respond in writing, either electronically or on paper, while you're at the height of your anger. When feeling angry, immerse yourself in a different activity to get your mind off of it. Give yourself time to put the issue in perspective. Most of the time, the message you would have written won't be worth your own continued aggravation, as anger only destroys you, not your opponent.

Tapper's Tip #10

A memo filled with venomous language should not be permitted in the workplace. Its author should be forced to "take it back." Your disciplinary policy should cover this kind of situation, and go so far as requiring termination (no matter what the rank) for the disrespect it shows to co-workers.

The Loose Cannon Roundup

So, now that you've seen these behavioral traits, you can appreciate that one person may have mixed traits that cross over to other loose cannon types. How many of these loose cannons are in your company? Do you identify with any of them? If so, you should discover enough in these pages to want to change your ways or face the risk that what you think you're doing as "protection" will backfire somewhere down the road.

Let's summarize some key points:

♦ Stay aware! Look at the e-mails you get each day with an eye for these traits in their authors. Look not only at the content of the memos and the correspondence, but be aware of their tone. Do you spot these tendencies or traits from the messages?

♦ Pay particular attention to taking some action that discourages this kind of imprudent writing. If you are in a management position and receive an e-mail from one of these cannons, do something about the inaccuracies, and stay focused on the status of the final "record."

◆ When a memo makes a dire prediction, or alerts you to a potentially dangerous condition, be aware of "subjectivity" in the description. Is this only an "opinion" being expressed? Or is it based on proven facts? Or a number of assumptions not expressed by the writer?

◆ Don't let a memo containing erroneous assumptions or wrong facts stand without response. I don't suggest a lengthy response by e-mail or written memo. You don't want to build a dialogue in writing on the issue. Question the assumptions made and suggest a meeting to discuss the issues further. And don't record or take minutes of the meeting. Unless major clarification and mutual agreement has occurred, think twice before memorializing the meeting results in writing.

◆ If the employee's opinion is based on proven facts that are not subject to question, invite further discussion. Do this in person to address the concerns, but certainly not by another e-mail or memo. Tackle the problems that do arise. Don't gloss over them and don't cover them up. Give them the attention they need. Delegate the issues needing resolution to an appropriate manager and make sure you follow-up.

◆ In general, when you have employees with the traits of loose cannons, encourage discussion by telephone or in-person, instead of through e-mails or memos on paper.

◆ Develop a corporate culture built on demonstrated commitment to integrity and fair dealing with employees and outsiders to foster a respectful working environment. The executive officers must be role models who continually show this commitment through sincerity in all that they do. Only then can a company foster an atmosphere where employees are free to discuss their concerns, without feeling the need to "protect" themselves in e-mail or on paper.

◆ When employees feel that no one in upper management "listens" to them, resentment and cynicism take hold. The ill-will spreads like a contagion and honest communication ceases. Each party thinks the other has an ulterior motive, and no one ever believes that all the cards are on the table. This is the environment that breeds discontent and encourages the loose cannons to show their familiar traits. It's also the breeding ground for a houseful of smoking guns.

Chapter 2

Rules of Engagement

How "the other side" invades your fortress

Picture this:

You're the CEO and your in-house attorney, Lyle Lawman, has just called to tell you your company has been served with papers as a defendant in a new lawsuit. The plaintiff is the company that bought your old manufacturing facility, with ten acres, for $150 million a year ago. The Complaint alleges that, before the sale, your company concealed important facts about its "improper" disposal of chemical wastes that contaminated subsurface soil, and had they known about this, they would not have closed the deal.

As CEO, you invite Lawman to your office to learn more about the situation and take a look at the actual Complaint. You read it and respond, *"This is bullshit! They've got buyer's remorse and are trying to squeeze us to get some money back. We had chemical discharges two years before the sale, but we cleaned them up, so there wasn't any reason to disclose them. File a motion and get this damned thing dismissed as a frivolous claim."*

"We'll do what we can," says Lawman, "but I think there's enough information in the Complaint that will prevent a court from dismissing it at this stage. The Court will allow the plaintiff a reasonable time for discovery to see what turns up in support of the allegations. In the meantime, we'll need to review your records, and those records of other officers and employees who had anything to do with the sale or the management of the property from the time our company originally purchased it in 1986 until the date of the sale to the plaintiff. That includes all of your old diaries and calendars—if you've kept them—your appointment books, and any correspondence files related in any way to the old property."

"That's ridiculous," you say. "They're filled with personal information. I meant to throw them away years ago, but for some reason never got around to it." "Well," says Lawman, "one thing's for sure: you can't get rid of them now because once litigation has begun, you can't destroy what could be potential evidence related in any way to the issues involved. If you do, you'll face severe penalties too costly to even talk about.

"Our preliminary review of archived files at the warehouse," says Lawman, "shows over 3000 storage boxes with related material. If we had adopted a document retention policy years ago that would have required document clean-out at designated intervals, we might have had only 100 boxes. Now we'll need a whole team of people to start looking at this stuff."

That isn't all, as Lawman tries to nonchalantly break some more news: *"The Plaintiff's lawyer obtained a court Order restraining all employees who had any involvement in the management or sale of the property from using their computers for the next 48 hours. That includes you. It allows the plaintiff's computer expert to make mirror-image copies of all of the information on our hard drives and the company's back-up servers to preserve all files and e-mails."*

"Are they nuts?" you shoot back, like a cat threatened by a predator. *"I'm not closing down my computer, and I'm not giving them my e-mails and correspondence. There's a lot of personal stuff on there as well as confidential company memos."*

"I hear you," says Lawman, *"but this is a court order and if you don't comply you'll be in contempt of court, which brings other sanctions. Their computer experts can tell if anything's been 'saved' or 'deleted' from here on, so I'm advising you to comply to avoid cries of foul play. They want to preserve the status quo of files. Before turning over the copies of the drives and tapes, we'll review the information to see if there are attorney-client privileged communications we can protect from disclosure, and anything else we can exclude as "not relevant" to the issues. But,that means we have to look at everything, including everyone's stored e-mails, and that's a monumental job ahead of us."*

Incredulous, you respond, *"Do you realize that I have over a thousand e-mails on my computer that I've read but never deleted! What about the rest of our management team? How many do you think they have? This could take forever!"*

"I know," says Lawman, *"and don't forget the back-up tapes that our information technology department has in storage, because they have to be reviewed also. The I.T. people have been backing up our system once a week for several years. There are hundreds of thousands of e-mails and documents on those tapes alone. Nothing is categorized to alert us to their topic, or to their confidential or privileged status, so we have to look at each one. We'll have to assemble a team of paralegals and lawyers to collect the information and coordinate the process. I'll send memos out throughout the departments to see who had anything to do with the old property, and advise them not to delete any e-mails or other documents that have anything to do with it."*

Lawman swallows hard, and adds, *"I have to tell you one more thing, which you're not going to like."* *"Go ahead,"* you say, *"what can be worse than this colossal intrusion on privacy?"* *"Do you have a home computer or laptop that you use for company business, even occasionally?"* he queries.

"Yes, I do," you reply, *"and so do all of our other key management people. We all use our e-mail system through remote access to our network."*

"Well," says Lawman, who tries to put this as delicately as he can, knowing your disdain for lawsuits, *"the court order requires that plaintiff's forensic expert be allowed to inspect and copy the hard drives, floppy disks, and any other electronic storage media from home computers and laptops of every person 'who now does or ever has done' company business through a remote access connection to our company's network. It's limited to those employees—which includes you—who had any connection with the sale or operation of the old property."*

Your face turns beet red and your muscles tighten while you blurt out enough epithets to make Lawman uneasy enough to be sure your office door is closed. Your mind flashes back to the personal information on the hard drive of your home computer, and the trail of Internet sites that either you or your teenage son might have visited over the past several months. You regain your senses and look Lawman directly in the eyes, as a lion would look at his prey just before the kill—a look he's seen on you very rarely in his twelve years with the company—and roar, *"Read my lips! The answer is...NOT! NA-DA! N-O! That [expletive deleted] plaintiff's lawyer has crossed the line. I don't care how many hoops you have to jump through, but you'd better make sure they don't get their way! File whatever you have to and get that [expletive deleted] court order quashed! I have a constitutional right to privacy and they have no right to demand such an intrusion. Tell their [expletive deleted] lawyer that she's messing with the wrong person, and I'll fight her to the bitter end!"*

With that outburst, Lawman, knowing when not to push his luck, leaves as quietly as he can. During a brief moment, he thinks about his own survival, and wonders, *"How in hell am I going to pull this one off?"* He runs to the phone and calls the company's outside defense counsel who has been engaged to defend the case,and starts strategizing on how to accomplish your directive. Counsel advises Lawman that he'll file the motion papers but it will probably be a losing battle, confirming what Lawman already suspected (and feared). He also adds some more advice —that Lawman's CEO has no such "constitutional right" in this context, and the discovery requested by the plaintiff is all permissible in the court's rules of procedure in this jurisdiction.

The truth is...

This scene is not just a fantasy. It's the "basic stuff" of litigation, and it pits your company as the defendant against the invading plaintiffs and their trial lawyers. The demands made for discovery of your information and the scope of what they can rightfully obtain are all within written rules known as "Rules of Civil Procedure" (what I'm referring to as the "rules of engagement").

Although we call it "civil" procedure, it oftentimes is less than civil. Let's face it, litigation is War! Call it what you want, but when you're served with a lawsuit, you have adversaries who want your money and whatever else they can get. Maybe, that "else" is to gain a competitive advantage, blemish or ruin the company's reputation through "bad" image publicity, tarnish your popular brand, obtain a court-order that requires you to restructure operations, or, get the court to impose fines and penalties for violations.

The "rules" are, essentially, the outline of how the war is to be conducted—the "fair play" or "civil" structure of it all. Each state has its own court system and its own rules as does the federal judicial system for the federal courts. As you'll see, depending on the degree of aggressiveness of plaintiffs' trial lawyers, it can get ugly and invasive.

Litigation is also a costly event. And you have no control over who decides to start it or when they choose to attack. That's why it's so important to be ready to beat them back at their own game, as their strategy is to pick, probe, and plunder the evidence in your own files, your own archives, and your own physical facilities to force you into surrender. You'd better have a commander-in-chief who's been in the trenches and knows how to plan and manage your litigation defense strategy with the most advantage, including how to keep your costs under control. The last thing you want is to discover in your own fortress a bunch of smoking guns that pin your defense to the wall, leaving you with nothing but surrender terms (desperate offers to settle) to get them to go away. But before you can appreciate the steps you should take to strengthen your defenses to reduce your smoking gun potential, you need to know where to look, and that comes from knowing how intrusive a plaintiff's invasion can get during the litigation process.

The tools and methods of discovery allow for an all-out assault on your company's information infrastructure. If there's any solace to this, the rules work the same for each side. If your company is the defendant, it, too, can act just as aggressively against the plaintiff's archives. In many situations, though, your company will have more to lose in exposing your own inside information than what you'll gain from a plaintiff's files.

Most of the cost of civil litigation is spent in the pre-trial discovery phase. The company's total bill will be directly proportionate to the aggressiveness of the parties, the number of parties, the claims and defenses raised on each side, the need for outside experts (and how many), how resistant each side is to the other's advances, the numbers of depositions that are taken, and how often you need the court to interpret, enforce, modify, or resolve disputes over the rules.

The rules actually allow the other side to legally get inside your files, get their hands on your confidential papers, and almost everything you've ever done, said or written. The depth of this probe is what's called the "scope of discovery."

When the plaintiffs' commandos (their trial lawyers) come bursting through the company's doors, your documents and deeds don't have to become the white flag of surrender. If you apply what you learn in these chapters, with your counsel's help, you'll be meeting your future adversaries with a more confident posture, ready to win the battle.

The battle begins

Once your company receives the plaintiff's Complaint which is filled with allegations of how and why the defendant has "wronged" the plaintiff, the battle has begun, and the company has a designated amount of time to "return fire" by filing its formal response, appropriately called an "Answer." The Answer usually denies the allegations the plaintiff has made and asserts the company's defenses to defeat the charges. Both sides then begin a period of pre-trial "discovery," which can usually vary from 90 to 180 days, depending on the court and the state where the case has been filed. (Note: In really complex cases, the pre-trial discovery period can go on for more than a year based on motions that each side typically files to extend the time.)

Since many of the states model their rules on the federal court system's rules, we'll use the federal court rules as our guide, too.

The scope of discovery: how much does the "other side" get to see?

The question of "scope"—the extent to which a plaintiff can probe into your company's inner sanctum—has to do with "relevance." If what the plaintiff asks to see, inspect, or copy has any relevance to the claims raised in the lawsuit or to any of the issues raised by your defense, it's fair game for discovery. Even if what they want has no direct relevance, the rules allow them to search and probe for anything that "appears reasonably calculated to lead to the discovery of admissible evidence."

What "leads" the trial lawyers to the stuff they want is "the paper trail" you and your colleagues leave with memos, e-mails, names of people mentioned in them, and cross-references to other documents, meetings, or transactions. One memo leads them to a person, and that person's files get reviewed, and information in those files leads to even more travels through the labyrinth of trails. That's how the paper trail comes alive!

Some jurisdictions don't measure "relevance" by just looking at whether the information wanted has anything to do with the actual claims or defenses raised by either side; they allow discovery as to anything relevant to "the subject matter" of the whole lawsuit, a much broader scope. For example, if a plaintiff claims your company misrepresented or concealed facts in one specific advertisement, relevance as to "claim" would be limited to information regarding that particular advertisement, while relevance as to the "subject matter" would allow discovery of information about all of your advertisements in general.

What kind of evidence can be discovered?

As to the "kinds" of evidence either party can see or obtain, there's virtually no limit. Here are some examples:

    ◆   Business records, calendars, diaries, notes, drafts of documents, signed originals of documents, faxes, memos, correspondence, invoices, purchase orders, financial information (including bank records), photographs, audio tapes, video tapes, blueprints, designs, and formulas... just to name some, and all tangible items such as furniture, equipment, products, tools, and parts.

    ◆   If real estate or a building is involved, each side is entitled to photograph and inspect all aspects of either.

    ◆   If products are involved, each side can take samples and send them to laboratories for testing, and if you have an allegedly defective product, the product can be inspected and tested to determine the location or cause of the defect.

◆   If a person's mental status is at issue, a party can even apply to the court for an Order requiring the person to undergo psychological tests and examinations. In personal injury cases, a defendant has the right to require the allegedly injured plaintiff to undergo a physical exam by an independent doctor chosen by the defendant.

On the electronic side, a party can demand inspection and copying of hard drives, back-up tapes and drives, floppy disks, CD-ROMs, and any other electronic storage medium, including personal digital assistants, laptop computers and their storage devices. This includes copies of files stored on these media, such as e-mails, word-processed documents, spreadsheets, databases, and any other kinds of files you might have.

Tapper's Tip #11

Companies are most vulnerable to an attack on their electronic files because so much is stored by computer, with few or no controls on what gets stored. The trial lawyers know it and are going after them like raiders of the lost ark!

Tapper's Tip #12

If you use your computer at home for work-related purposes, even partially, that, too, is vulnerable to discovery of all files on the hard drive, disks, or CD-ROMs, including e-mails and, in some cases, information as to the sites you have visited on the Internet.

As to getting information from questioning people, either side can demand oral testimony of the other's employees, including officers, right on up to the CEO and members of the Board of Directors. And you don't have to be a current employee. Former employees are fair game. In short, anybody who has any information within the "scope" of the pre-trial discovery rules can be pursued and interrogated.

The myth of "confidentiality"

In my presentations to business groups on the topics in this book, audiences react with the most surprise to what I call "the myth of confidentiality. " Most people think that if a document is stamped "confidential" at the top, that's enough to keep it from outsiders' eyes as if it were "protected" property. NOT SO! That's all a myth!

Tapper's Tip #13

For pre-trial discovery purposes, consider almost everything in your paper files, computer drives, electronic storage media, and work surroundings as discoverable by the other side. In discovery, your actions in the workplace are the same as working in a glass house with no drapes or blinds.

Confidential documents are fully discoverable (required to be produced) in the litigation arena, except for those documents cloaked with the special status of either "attorney-client privilege" or "attorney work product" (which we'll discuss in the next section). For the most part, if a document is not in one of these special status categories, it doesn't matter that it's "confidential" in the pre-trial discovery rules of engagement.

For internal company purposes, all of those e-mail messages, or memos and letters you carefully label as "personal," or "confidential," or "for your eyes only," qualify for special handling among your colleagues to keep their audience limited and restricted. But when it comes to a lawsuit against your company, if the subject matters you speak about in those "confidential" messages are "relevant" to the issues in the suit, everything is up for grabs. It doesn't matter a hoot that they're confidential. You'll have to produce them unless you can convince a court you're entitled to protection from disclosure because of some protected privilege, or a need to protect a trade secret.

If that doesn't give you some pause for drafting your messages more carefully, I don't know what will!

Tapper's Tip #14

Although confidential documents are discoverable in litigation, don't give up on protecting them in-house. Until there's a lawsuit demanding them, you still need to keep the information they contain from falling into the wrong hands inside the company or from an unauthorized and improper release to the public. Restricted distribution of information has an important security value, particularly for proprietary property and trade secrets. In public companies, securities' laws and regulations even require special handling of "insider" information.

Attorney-client privileged communications

The attorney-client privilege is one of non-disclosure, and it's reserved for communications between an attorney and a client where either the client is seeking, or the attorney is giving, legal advice. In the corporate world, that could mean an e-mail between your in-house counsel and you, in whatever official role or capacity you maintain for the company, provided it involves legal advice. But, as we'll see in Chapter 8 on attorney-client privilege, the privilege to withhold disclosure is a fragile perk that can easily be lost ("waived") through misunderstanding, or lax handling procedures, by either the "client," or the attorney.

If you claim certain documents are "privileged," you have to provide a list to the other side's attorneys which describes the nature of the documents you refuse to turn over. That list has to have enough description, short of revealing the actual contents, so the other side can determine if there's merit to challenge your right not to disclose them. During these challenges your company's procedures for protecting the confidentiality of the documents are put to the test. Should they fall short, the privilege of non-disclosure is lost, and the other side gets to see the contents.

One more type of document gets protection from disclosure, and that's the document that an attorney or an agent of the attorney or company prepares "in anticipation of litigation." This is known as "work product" and the courts have been willing to protect these papers, particularly if they contain the mental impressions and notes of attorneys. Typically, "attorney work product" relates to notes that your attorney or his agent takes when either person conducts an investigation in the face of threatened litigation. These papers are usually attorney-directed and controlled, and there are many legal technicalities that the company's attorney has to meet to keep this special status (which, also, is not guaranteed). As such, we'll leave it for your company's attorney to worry about, beyond our focus here.

Protective orders

So what about trade secrets, such as customer lists, manufacturing processes, and blueprints or designs and other proprietary information? They, too, are discoverable, provided the plaintiff can show they're relevant to the claims, or "reasonably calculated" to lead to the discovery of "relevant" evidence. However, the rules allow for your attorneys to apply to the court for a "protective" order that can limit the circumstances of the disclosures.

The protection available through "protective orders" depends on the "need" you show to the court. These orders can include protections ranging from not allowing the other side to see the information to setting certain limitations on how it's to be seen, copied, or distributed. You might even get the court to change the method of discovery. For example, perhaps the other side is a competitor, and you don't want their engineering people to inspect or review your manufacturing processes, which you consider to be proprietary. In this case, the court may order that an independent third party be designated to review the process, with results reportable only to the other side's attorney. It may also restrict the plaintiff's attorney from disclosing it to officers or other business people on the plaintiff's side.

The rules allow leeway to customize a protective order to the special needs of the parties to the litigation, but although a court has wide discretion in what it can allow, the discretion is tightly exercised. If you seek a protective order, you've got to have good reasons that convince the court that more harm than good would come if the protection were not granted.

Tapper's Tip #15

Civil trials are not soap opera dramas where the surprise witness bursts into the courtroom to save the day. The rules of engagement are designed to avoid surprises for either side and to discourage the withholding of evidence. The difference between winning and losing a case is often related to how thoroughly and aggressively each side uses all of the tools and methods available (through the "rules") to find the evidence on the other side. Rather than restrict documents from view, courts usually favor "liberal" and "open" discovery.

Tools and methods for discovery: an arsenal of weapons

In civil litigation, each side has a wide choice of "weapons" (tools and methods) available through the rules to find and get the evidence needed to win the case. The three most commonly used are the Notice to Produce Documents and Things ("Notice to Produce"), Interrogatories, and Depositions.

Notice to Produce

The Notice To Produce is a powerful weapon because it requires you to produce virtually anything within the scope of discovery, from paper files to electronic media to tangible objects, all of which can be copied, inspected, measured, surveyed, photographed, or tested—you name it!

Consider, however, that in terms of hard drives, CD-ROMs, floppy disks, and magnetic back-up tapes, and the thousands of e-mails and millions of pages of documents that can reside on these storage devices, the task to review these documents and then produce them is enormous. How many hours would it take, for example, to sift through thousands of pages to find and remove the special material for which you might want to obtain a "protective order"? When that's done, you still have to sort through the rest of the information to deliver what's "relevant" in response to the Notice to Produce.

Can you now begin to see the cost of litigation in terms of labor hours, alone, devoted to document production? I can tell you from years of experience that the process is not just a law department function. It disrupts everyone in the organization who has anything to do with the subject matter of the lawsuit as each person sifts through his or her own files, diaries, computer drives, and the storage boxes of old files delivered to the office from the archive-storage warehouse. And all of this is happening while employees are trying to stay on target to achieve revenue-goals and fulfill marketing initiatives.

In many cases, the party obligated to produce their paper and electronic files, and the tangible objects for discovery, bears the cost of compliance without reimbursement by the party demanding it. The cost can be in the thousands, and could reach hundreds of thousands of dollars in larger companies. Sounds crazy, doesn't it? But that's life in the civil litigation world, and that's how lawsuits can get so costly and detrimental to your financial well-being, particularly if they're not smartly managed by professionals experienced in litigation management.

Tapper's Tip #16

To reap huge savings in time and labor costs of complying with future discovery requests, you should establish a code system that identifies e-mails and word-processed files, before they are stored, with labels such as "privileged," "proprietary," "trade secret," or "confidential." Make the code searchable with a "key word" search in your operating system so you can quickly find the electronic documents that need your attention during a discovery production request.

Forensic experts: Rebuilding your old files

Today, "electronic discovery" (where trial lawyers seek to find your smoking guns in your computer drives and all other similar storage-media devices) has spawned a burgeoning field of computer experts who make themselves available for hire to attorneys. They reconstruct the hard drives from employees' computers and the back-up drives of a company's servers to find not only the current files, including e-mails, that are stored there, but to detect old, deleted files that have not yet been overwritten.

It may be hard to believe, but when you delete a file, it still remains stored on the original drive or disk until you overwrite the space it occupies with a newly saved file. (I'll give you the details of how this works in Chapter 3.) By finding the old remnants of these files, many "old" e-mails can be resurrected to your, and the company's, surprise. Watch out! This is an extremely vulnerable area where smoking guns are harbored.

Boot camps for lawyers: Commando training for your hard drives

At least once a month, I receive a brochure advertising a workshop or seminar for trial attorneys on how to conduct electronic discovery. At these events, they're admonished to use the tactic of obtaining a restraining order at the front end of a lawsuit to allow their expert to download a mirror-image of hard drives and back-up tapes before a defendant has a chance to "save" new files that might overwrite the old or "deleted" ones. Once mirror-images of the drives and tapes have been made, the company can continue using its computers because the experts will complete their search-and-find missions on the "mirror-image" copies by putting their special software programs to work, reconstructing the remnants of files that have been "deleted" but not yet overwritten.

Should a "deleted" file that's been retrieved be used as evidence against you?

Some interesting issues arise from discovery of "deleted" files that have been resurrected. Should they be admissible as evidence at trial? Should a "deleted" message or file be treated the same as a paper file that has been thrown away? And what if the file you deleted was an attorney-client privileged one? Does it lose the "privilege" of non-disclosure because you "threw it away" by deleting it? If you throw away an attorney-client privileged communication in paper form by simply throwing it in a wastebasket without first shredding it, the memo may lose its privileged status because you didn't act prudently to protect its confidentiality. (Anyone can pick it out of the trash and read it.) If you can "shred" documents, in the electronic sense, with available software programs that fully erase the remnants of deleted files by overwriting them, a court may consider your failure to use such programs, when deleting a privileged communication, the same way as it would for a paper document thrown away, whole, in the wastebasket.

Unfortunately, there are no definitive answers to these issues, although there are cogent arguments on both sides of the battle fronts. Be assured that as trial lawyers and the courts get more familiar with electronic discovery and its intrusiveness, these issues will be fought by both sides in future battles. It's likely that courts will differ on the outcomes depending on the facts of each case.

Tapper's Tip #17

Software programs are available to overwrite the spaces occupied by deleted files so the old remnants cannot be reconstructed. If your company doesn't already have them to "clean up" all the files you delete, including e-mails, it should be investigating their purchase and application without delay.

Interrogatories

Interrogatories (think of the word, "interrogate," which is "to question") are an inexpensive tool because they're written questions sent to you or your company to be answered in writing, but under oath as to the truth and accuracy of the answers. The questions that can be asked are limited only by the "scope" of the discovery rules.

The more commonly asked questions sift out information as to whether documents exist, and if so, their location, the kinds of electronic storage a company uses, the software programs it utilizes, including its operating system, whether it has backup servers and, if so, all of the details concerning them, plus names, titles, and addresses of people who have any knowledge of the issues raised in the lawsuit, and the factual details that your side asserts in support of your defenses.

Background information to find the paper trails

The plaintiff's lawyers use the interrogatories to get background information about your company and its internal structure. They use them for "leads" on where they might find some "gems" for future discovery. For example, in a premises liability case against a hotel, where a guest tripped on a stairway, an interrogatory (a single question) might ask you to give the names and addresses of all people who have tripped on that same stairway over the last five years. If there were routine incident reports filled out at the time of the incidents, it will request you to attach copies of them, or make them available for inspection. The plaintiff's investigator may then follow the "paper trails" of those incident reports which will reveal not only the names of former guests who were injured, but those of employees who wrote up the reports and had knowledge of the prior conditions of the stairway.

Before returning the written responses to these interrogatories, management will usually consult with the company's attorneys. It's no secret that each side's attorneys usually wordsmith the choice of language for these responses, and most of the time, they obtain the information needed from management and other employees, and actually complete the responses for management to sign.

Tapper's Tip #18

Interrogatories are a useful tool in laying the groundwork to find paper trails and discover what each side's position is on the issues in dispute. Be sure the answers you give in writing are consistent with the testimony that not only you expect to give, but that other known witnesses will give, when their depositions take place. Each witness who will be involved should be made aware of the interrogatories, and how the company responded to them, as a basic preparation, before entering the lion's den to give oral testimony to the other side.

Depositions

Depositions are a powerful, but costly, tool in the trial lawyers' arsenal. This involves meeting in person with your and the other side's attorney to answer questions, under oath, asked of you by the attorney who called for the deposition. A court stenographer takes down every question and answer by silently typing the words each person speaks on a little machine, in shorthand style. The questions and answers are later translated from shorthand to English onto regular size paper and bound into a booklet which is called a "transcript." Nowadays, a computer scans the notes and translates them for print-out.

The deposition usually takes place in an attorney's conference room or in a hotel meeting room reserved for that purpose. Usually, your company's attorney will prepare you ahead of time on what to expect, and to familiarize you with questions to be anticipated. During the actual deposition, you're "on your own" to answer what is asked, and everything you say is taken down by the stenographer, even the "um's" and "eh's."

It's a challenging experience to respond to questions at random by the plaintiff's attorney who you know is trying to get you to say things detrimental to your company's defense and helpful to his client's case.

Tapper's Tip #19

Whatever you say in the deposition can be used against you and the company for whom you're testifying at the time of trial. It's treated the same as testimony would be, if you were giving it in court.

Video-taped Deposition: Smile You're On Camera!

The side that calls for your deposition also has the right to have it videotaped. Not only does it record your words, but it captures each smile or grimace, and every nervous twitch, too! The video camera sits on a tripod at the opposite end of the conference room table, focused directly, and continuously, on you.

In the same manner as a written transcript of your deposition can be used against you in trial, so can any portion of the videotaped deposition. You know how first impressions control your like or dislike of a person upon meeting for the first time? Jurors form the same impressions when they see you on a television screen in the courtroom for the first time. Your outward appearance, attitude, temper, and speech are all significant and influential in a videotaped deposition.

An experienced and aggressive trial lawyer can make very effective use of your video image in court, particularly when the goal is to discredit your testimony with a smoking gun memo that you may have authored several years back. Suppose, for example, you were asked in your videotaped deposition what you thought of the CEO of your company, and you responded that you thought she was "competent and focused." In an internal memo, however, a few years back, after a heated disagreement, you sent a memo to a close colleague and referred to this CEO in a notation in the margin as "an inexperienced, incompetent, and mean S.O.B." Using today's technical capabilities, the trial lawyer can project a split screen T.V. image in the courtroom where the incendiary phrase in your own writing is enlarged and highlighted on the right half of the screen, while your video image and voice referring to the CEO as "competent and focused" are on the left side. The impact is powerful. Your credibility is on "wipe-out." Not only did the jurors get their first impression of you when you took the stand; they now have a lasting impression which they'll carry into the jury room at the final hour.

How long can they hold you hostage in a deposition?

Lucky for you, you won't need a pillow and an overnight bag—that is, in most cases. The federal rules now impose limitations on how long a lawyer can keep you in the deposition. The limit is one day of seven hours, which means seven hours of testimony, not including lunch time and other breaks. The catch is that a federal district court may extend the limit, or the parties can agree to a different set of "caps" on timing. Extensions may be justified if a person has an English language problem and needs a translator, or if there's a large volume of documents to go through, or the events involved span a long period of time that cannot be covered in the established limit.

Testimony at trial

Remember, the deposition is a discovery tool where the other side asks questions without really knowing in advance what your response will be. They're looking for trails to find the ultimate smoking gun, while at the same time, setting "in concrete" your version of the facts as you know them so you don't change your story by the time of trial. If you do, you will have created your own smoking gun on the spot.

Assuming your availability, you may be required to testify in open court during the trial. It doesn't matter that you've given your testimony already by deposition; the trial is a whole new battlefield. By that time, the attorney who asked you the questions at your deposition knows (or, at least, expects) how you will respond to them when he's ready. So, the questions at trial are designed to elicit the answers from you that he expects. But don't rely on him asking them in the same way or same order because if he's good, he won't. It's a game of catching you off base, a way to combat memorized preparation. The experienced trial lawyer will weave what he expects you will say into the theme of his client's story, just at the right place, for the most impact.

If the answer you give is contrary to something you said at your deposition, you'll find the transcript of your deposition "in your face" to show the jury your contradictions while under oath. That contradiction can discredit the trustworthiness of your testimony, not only for yourself, but for your company on whose behalf you appeared. If you're caught unaware and ill-prepared, you could be wounded by your own smoking gun—the deposition transcript.

Tapper's Tip #20

If your deposition has been taken during pre-trial discovery and you are required to testify at the trial, don't ever go to the trial without having obtained a copy of the transcript of your deposition well in advance and studied it for the questions asked and the responses you gave. Be prepared and know what you've already said before taking the witness stand in the courtroom.

The trial lawyers' document bank

Plaintiffs' trial lawyers have now put the Internet to widespread use as a litigation document "bank." Associating in specialty groups, they've created Web sites that house "discovery" documents collected from litigation (mostly product liability) against big companies and industries. These are "members-only" sites where lawyers contemplating a lawsuit against, let's say, Ford Motor Company, can join the site (membership is strictly controlled to be sure you're not a defense lawyer on the "enemy" side) and search the documents produced by Ford in the cases it defended around the country. Members can access transcripts of depositions of company officials or read the testimony they gave at trials, examine the testimony of experts the company has used in its defense, and review engineering documents, e-mail messages, memos, correspondence, and any other item of interest from the prior lawsuits.

Every smoking gun in prior lawsuits either produced by the companies, themselves, or acquired independently through other sources, is on file! Members can even enter search words or phrases, such as "fuel tank design," and access only the portions of documents that mention those words or phrases. The documents are categorized by company name, product involved (Ford Explorer, for example), and individual employee names (for documents authored by that person, or for those where the person's name is mentioned, or the transcript of testimony previously given by that person).

One of the groups is known as Attorneys Information Exchange Group, a cooperative of lawyers who share the documents they acquire through discovery. Each member of the co-op forwards documents to a central Web site repository (a "bank") which is accessible by all other members. *Business Week* magazine called it a "Library of Congress for the internal paperwork of dozens of companies" in a fascinating article which was their cover story, "The Litigation Machine," in its June 29, 2001 issue. Other similar groups are fostered by The American Trial Lawyers' Association (ATLA) which sponsors the ATLA Exchange. Lawyers in these groups have formed more concentrated subgroups that focus on particular kinds of cases against specific companies, such as parking lot assaults or injuries from aisle obstructions at Walmart stores. According to *Business Week*, ATLA has 61 litigation groups "covering everything from automatic-door malfunctions to defective toys to tap-water burns."

The sensational headlines about the Firestone tire recall (and debacle) generated hundreds of new lawsuits. It didn't take long before the "exchange" groups formed new Web sites with litigation "packets," or kits, that gave a plaintiff's lawyer everything needed to start a suit against the company. It included a detailed history of the tire company's knowledge of problems and sample complaints from previously filed tread separation cases that were instructive as to which parties to name as defendants. A member can look up memos and correspondence that had been produced from the company's archives in other product liability cases, with particular emphasis on the smoking gun memos, plus a directory of links to other Web sites for additional helpful information.

To be sure, defense lawyers also have their "exchange" groups, and, with the same detail as the plaintiffs, they keep track of the experts that plaintiffs' trial lawyers have used in their suits against companies, as well as information on trial tactics that have worked, and not worked, against plaintiffs and their experts.

Keeping track of what you give up in discovery

What this all shows is that a company must be meticulous in tracking the information it produces in the discovery process and keeping account of the information for consistency in future responses. Companies that are subject to a large number of lawsuits should keep a "production document bank" (as a matter of necessity) that organizes and categorizes the information produced in each suit.

Given the databases maintained by plaintiffs' trial lawyers in these frequently targeted companies, it's easy to spot when you haven't produced "all" of the relevant documents in the company's archives in response to their Notice to Produce. When that happens, trial lawyers file motions in court to impose sanctions on your company for failure to obey the rules.

The court has a wide discretion to fashion appropriate sanctions against a party that doesn't play by them. It's detrimental to your company to be on the defensive end of motions for sanction on a frequent basis, as it lends a perception of your company as a dishonest player. In future court cases, when your defense counsel needs the aid of the court on your behalf, and the relief is in the sole discretion of the trial judge, your counsel may have a more difficult time persuading the judge to see things your way.

And, above all, the existence of these "litigation machines" shows that if you create a smoking gun and your company produces it, as required, it will have a life well beyond one lawsuit. So long as the trial lawyers maintain their document "banks"—and you can be assured they will—your smoking gun will remain "on deposit" until the issues it involves are no longer useful in any lawsuit against your company. That, my friend, can be a long, long time, and a heavy burden to bear for not only you, but your company.

Chapter

3

E-mails and E-files

The electronic world of smoking guns

ALERT! Plaintiff's trial lawyers have landed their troops inside your company's fortress. They want smoking guns. Where do they search?

First place: In employees' E-mails.

Next: In all other electronically-stored files.

Their game plan and objective: To secure access to your computers and their hard drives, and locate all floppy disks, CD ROMs, and back-up tapes, before newly-saved files can overwrite the existing data.

In addition to e-mails, almost every letter, memo, or report is typed on a computer's keyboard, and stored electronically as a word-processed document, spreadsheet, or database before it's printed out as a hard copy. As a convenient communication tool within a company where large numbers of employees are widespread in departments and divisions, electronic messaging is unequaled for speed and response times. Unfortunately, it's also unequaled in the minefield of traps it creates for those who don't think about its dangers.

E-mails top the list as the single most troublesome area for increasing a company's potential exposure to liability. Other electronically-stored files, such as word-processed documents, are a close second, particularly because of the ease of accumulating them in multiple draft versions that never get deleted.

Nine E-World Traps

Let's explore my list of Nine E-World Traps that can catch you unaware in your use of e-mails, computer-based files, and the Internet. Each "trap" is named for its main topic:

1. Casual-Speak
2. Unsolicited Message
3. Closet Clutter
4. Back-up Archive
5. Deleting and Deluding
6. Runaway Message
7. Date-Time Tattoo
8. Interception
9. Snooping Eyes

1. The "Casual-Speak" Trap

The danger of e-mail is in its simplicity. E-mail communication is easy, convenient, and immediate. The very nature of it is casual—a conversational dialogue between friends, business colleagues in the workplace, and people outside the company. When typing an e-mail, you have the impression you're face-to-face with the person you're talking to, and although you're not, you still tend to write in the conversational style.

Ah, but beware! The casualness and simplicity of this system hides the beast within. You're not just passing conversation, you're creating a permanent record. As fast as your fingers can type the words, your message makes its way to the screen, and all you need do is click "Send," and it's done. There's little time to bother with proofreading before you send a message because that interrupts the rhythm and flow of what you feel in ordinary conversation. Many e-mails are written from "the gut." Oh, you might give a quick glance at the e-mail to be sure it says what you intended, but it's nothing close to real proofreading. Your response to reading it over is more reflexive than contemplative. You speak to the moment. But the "moment" can be forever, and your words might just as well be set in stone. Excuse me, but is the beast in sight yet?

In contrast, writing on paper makes you more circumspect. You can hold the paper, see and reflect on the words, and feel a sense of permanency that you don't get with e-mails. When you write on paper, you sign or initial it signifying personal approval of the contents. Before signing, you make changes, refine your thoughts, and polish the message because every letter you sign is a self-portrait that shows your grammar, style, tone, spelling acumen, and, ultimately, intellectual caliber. Like it or not, the recipients of your paper memos and letters form an impression of you from your writing, a perception that becomes reality in most of the business world.

On the other hand, e-mail perception is different because it's the "fast" medium for communication, as opposed to the "formal" medium of traditional writing. The "casual-speak trap" catches you when you lose sight of the permanency of your e-mail message, and the speed at which it can be distributed to others beyond your control.

What you say today in an e-mail, when read back at a different time and place, can prove quite embarrassing taken out of context, particularly when you're sitting in a courtroom and your opponent is reading your words out loud to a jury and you're squirming at the sound of them.

Tapper's Tip #21:

Write e-mails as if they will appear on the desk of the President and CEO of your company, and if you hold either office already, as if the Board of Directors will see them. Write as if every e-mail will one day be made public.

Tapper's Tip #22:

Never write in anger. When in an emotional state, STOP! Let the matter sit for 24 hours. Think and reflect. Consider what your reply will look and sound like six months or two years from now, when everyone is calm, and fences have been mended. Will it be embarrassing to read to strangers? When you're trying to convince a jury that you're a reasonable, rational, and likable person who handles people with care and sensitivity, will the e-mail support that impression? Does it exhibit leadership qualities that would warrant your promotion?

> **Tapper's Tip #23:**
>
> Treat e-mails like tattoos. Once they're "on" (having been sent to someone), they're impossible to erase (you can delete them from your computer, but can't control what the recipients do with them.). Be sure you can "live with them" (as in seeing them return to you in another context) before you send them.

2. The Unsolicited Message Trap

Despite company policy against it, humorous and off-color comments in the form of cartoons, one-liners, and anecdotes, make their way around the workplace. Sometimes they include photographs or references and links to pornographic Web sites. What may seem innocuous to some is the seed for a claim of hostile work environment or sexual harassment to others. Instead of a joke or cartoon, the e-mail exchange might contain a descriptive observation about a co-worker concerning an overweight appearance, or a sexy look. Then someone in the chain of distribution makes a comment on top of the original one, and others add some humorous (or personally harsh or sexually suggestive) new remarks. That's all it takes. It snowballs. And as it does, so do the potential smoking guns.

You may find yourself as the innocent receiver of these e-mail messages sent to you or forwarded from a well-liked co-worker or a colleague in another company. If you send off a fast reply that says, "Right on!" or "Really funny!...so true..." or "hahaha—that was a good one," you placate your friend, and maybe you try to top his joke or comment by adding one of your own. Trap time! This is enough to implicate you in approving the content of the messages. Like it or not, you're now a participant.

Tapper's Tip #24:

Just say "no" to e-mails you know are trouble. Avoid them, and unless you need to show them to a supervisor, get rid of them.

As you know from the "rules of engagement," all of your e-mail exchanges are discoverable in litigation. What if the gist of a lawsuit is against you or your company for sexual harassment, discrimination of some kind, or a hostile work environment based on incidents unrelated to your e-mails? Those e-mails you thought were funny at the time get paraded out as evidence to show the attitude of managers and employees in fostering an unfriendly work environment. If you weren't on the list before, you can be assured you'll be on plaintiff's list of whose deposition to take during the pre-trial discovery phase of the litigation. The downloaded messages are "paper trails" that help the other side gain the advantage.

Tapper's Tip #25:

Beware, if you're a government employee, because your e-mails may be subject to public disclosure under the Freedom of Information Act. Compose them as if you're writing to the public, because you are.

Interestingly, that's one of the reasons why President George W. Bush and Vice-President Dick Cheney, upon assuming their offices, stopped using e-mails to communicate with their daughters in college. Not surprisingly, they preferred not sharing their personal messages with the public.

Be on the alert when you next receive an e-mail. Question it this way: Can this be construed in a controversial way, or manipulated against me, if it were to show up in pre-trial discovery? If it can, you should count on a plaintiff's lawyer using it, when discovered, to gain whatever advantage she can. Remember: The biggest gains always come from your company's own files.

So, here's some advice when that next "e-mail grenade" gets lobbed over to your side:

♦ Don't reply to an e-mail that's inappropriate for the workplace, such as one containing off-color jokes, comments with sexist or racist undertones, messages that disparage religious beliefs, any language reflecting sexual overtones or interests, or any personal critiques of persons in the workplace.

♦ If this is an isolated instance, delete it.

♦ If it's not, print each one out, and then delete it from your desktop. Put the printouts into a confidential folder for the attention of the appropriate level of management, if needed. In a diplomatic way, inform the sender by phone or in person that you cannot respond to the e-mails because, in your opinion, they may have inappropriate connotations for the workplace. If the sender understands and stops sending the messages, discard the folder and be done with it. If, however, the response is negative, threatening, or antagonistic, and the e-mails still continue, present the folder to management for action and follow-up. If your e-mail program enables it, block out further e-mails from the sender.

I know this could be a delicate situation in any workplace in terms of relationships with co-workers. If you're in management and you received the e-mail from one of your staff members, your leadership authority should be sufficient to put an end to the behavior. Otherwise, if you can't amicably convince the sender of the inappropriateness of the e-mail content, you'll have to proceed with discretion and confidentiality at management levels. If this feels uncomfortable to you, remember this: You could be saving your department from a lengthy and costly involvement in the next employment lawsuit, and the savings might save someone's job (maybe your own) in the next round of cuts.

Tapper's Tip #26:

"No Gossip, No Bad-Mouth." Live by that credo in your e-mail exchanges. Save the "juicy" scuttlebutt and colorful talk for in-person conversations.

COMPANIES FIGHT BACK TO REDUCE LIABILITY EXPOSURE

The misuse of e-mails is a major problem for companies suffering liability for the e-mail activity of their employees.

Companies are fighting back by adopting e-mail and Internet usage policies that inform employees of the do's and don'ts of use. They're also using "filter" programs—software that blocks out unwanted words or phrases selected by the company as undesirable for e-mails. For example, a filter could block "cuss" words, racially derogatory references, and sexually explicit language from e-mails that employees send. This reduces the potential for inappropriate e-mails that may find their way into employment lawsuits alleging sexual harassment, hostile environment, or racial discrimination. These programs can alert an employee with a pop-up warning on his monitor whenever he uses the contraband words. Not only confined to e-mails, they're capable of providing a printed "record" that identifies violators and lists the words that were used, the date and time of use, and the files in which they appeared. Your company can use this information to monitor potential trouble spots before they become smoking guns.

Tapper's Tip #27:

As an employee, you're best advised to expect that your computer terminal, the computer equipment, and all messages and files you type, send, store, or receive, belong to the company. Use of the computer and the network system for personal matters should be considered prohibited activity, unless the company establishes specific exemptions for special circumstances. Don't be so naïve to think your "personal" messages are your private property when using company paid-for-and-supplied equipment and Internet access privileges.

These preventive risk management steps provide additional protection that reduces the risk of liability for wrongful employee actions. But the whole issue of privacy in the workplace is in its evolutionary stage, and courts can get creative in company vs. employee matters. Prudence requires that managers inform new employees at "new-hire" orientation, and current employees through on-screen messages at startup of e-mail access, that you have these policies in effect. Warn them not to expect privacy in using the company's computers for e-mails.

When your company enforces the rules, it stands a better chance of succeeding in court if it can show the rules were clear and made known to all of the employees who use the system and equipment owned and supplied by the company.

The reality is that companies, indeed, are taking these issues seriously. According to press reports in September, 2000, Dow Chemical Company fired over 20 employees and reprimanded over 200 others at its plant in Texas after an e-mail investigation disclosed that employees used the e-mail system to send graphical material depicting violence or sexually explicit situations. Dow is typical of many who have taken such steps to reduce their liability potential.

Although these policies and programs are useful in producing effective results, they'll produce friction and contempt when first introduced to employees who have otherwise been free to do as they pleased. Management's approach, and demonstrated commitment to enforcing its standards, will foretell the success or failure of the program.

Tapper's Tip #28:

Employees will "buy-in" to the need for usage controls on e-mails if you show them the consequences of inappropriate e-mail activity and the need for protecting the company, and themselves, from potential liability. Include all ranks of employees on management teams to participate in the development of these policies.

---

3. The "Closet Clutter" Trap

Just as the paper memos, company flyers, junk mail, and correspondence keep piling up in the In-box on your actual desk top, so do the e-mails on your desktop PC. The trap here is that you don't see them piling up so readily as you do the paper on your desk. Your on-screen desktop holds much more before you even begin to notice it's time for a "clean-out." It's not unusual to have over 400 e-mails just sitting in your e-mail program's Inbox, all having been read, but not deleted. The same goes for your Sent folder where you accumulate all the messages you sent, but never deleted. There's always a tendency to simply send the e-mail and pay no further attention to it, adding it to the already over-stuffed "Sent" folder. But if you don't pay attention to frequent and regularly-scheduled "clean-outs," the message trails keep accumulating to the point where they're so overwhelming in number you don't have the time to even begin to sift through them. Consequently, your electronic "closet" fills with clutter, some of which could be quite damaging if it had to be produced for pre-trial discovery.

Where are these incoming and outgoing messages actually stored? Although your old messages appear on your monitor when you enter your company's network to access your e-mails, the e-mails are actually residing on your company's main servers, not on your desktop PC, unless you downloaded them to your hard drive. All of the e-mails that employees receive and send take up a huge amount of memory capacity on the servers' hard drives. Every so often, your system administrator will require employees to clean-out all pending e-mails to free up needed space on the hard drives of the company's main servers. This helps to avoid unwanted and untimely system crashes.

If your company doesn't maintain its own computer network for e-mails, it relies on an Internet Service Provider (ISP) who provides access to either a paid commercial site, such as America Online® (www.aol.com) for e-mail service, or any of the numerous public e-mail hosts, such as Hotmail® (www.hotmail.com), Yahoo® (www.yahoo.com), and Lycos® (www.lycos.com), to name just a few. In that case, your e-mails are sitting on the servers of the company that's hosting the e-mail site. They allot a designated amount of memory space to each user for message activity before your "mailbox" is full and your e-mails get "returned to sender" as undeliverable. It's up to you to clear your mailbox, but until you do, your e-mails are sitting ducks for snoopers, hackers, and errant employees who maintain the public sites.

CLEAN-OUT: A DOUBLE-EDGED SWORD!

Depending on how you go about a "clean-out" or "purge" of old e-mails (both "sent" and "received"), you might be unknowingly breeding smoking guns and laying paper trails. Here's how it happens:

For those messages you feel you "have to keep," you'll usually save them to the hard drive on either your desktop or laptop, in a folder you might designate as "Archive" or some other name of choice. You might even download them to a portable disk where you can retrieve them later, or print them out to save as paper copies.

If you're under time constraints, and your company's administrator warns that on a designated date and time all e-mails on the server received within a certain time period will be deleted, you might feel compelled to download and save them all for review "later." You tell yourself that you'll have time later to decide what to save or delete. You know, of course, that when "later" comes, you'll have another 500 to 1,000 new messages accumulated. You'll never have the time to complete the review. So you do the same the next time around, and the system perpetuates itself as a virtual production factory for smoking guns. Your hard drive clutters up, or, if they were saved to disks, your portable disks pile up in your desk drawer. Welcome to the "closet clutter trap."

Unfortunately, you may not know you're in it until it's too late. When you least expect it, your law department, or the company's outside counsel, will one day inform you of a new lawsuit against the company (which can include you as a named defendant). Counsel will warn you to stop any destruction or alteration of "files," and that means paper and electronic ones, including all those disks of e-mail messages in your drawer.

Now just imagine:

Your company is served with a subpoena today that requires you to turn over all of your records for review. What do you have waiting for discovery in your office? Think about your e-mail messages on the company's servers and those in your desk drawer on portable disks, and the files on the hard drive of your desktop or laptop? I can bet there's enough gold inside to satisfy any plaintiff's trial lawyer. I can see him salivating already, in anticipation. Don't you think it's time to make time for clean-out...BEFORE you're taken by surprise?

Tapper's Tip #29:

Clean out your e-mail messages on a regular schedule, and if not on a daily basis, at least once a week. Immediately delete unneeded and unwanted e-mails to avoid clutter and save yourself from a potential "surprise attack" of a subpoena that could halt any further deletions.

Tapper's Tip #30:

Do not store e-mails unless they are essential to an ongoing project. Once the project is finished, consider deleting those e-mails that are no longer relevant. An e-mail usage and retention policy comes in handy here for your guidelines. Check to see if your company has one, and if not, encourage the powers-that-be to adopt one.

Tapper's Tip #31:

If you have drafts of old memos or letters where the"final" versions have already been sent, consider getting rid of all of the other versions. Delete them (after consulting with your company's attorney, to be sure there is no "legal" reason to keep them).

Tapper's Tip #32:

Follow your company's e-mail retention policy consistently and do not second-guess the rationale behind it. When in doubt as to "save or not to save," rely on the advice of your company's attorney. Just think, if it "hits the fan" after that, you can always say you relied on your attorney's advice, which is usually a viable defense!

Tapper's Tip #33:

Always consult with your in-house or outside counsel before destroying or altering any files. Once litigation has started, or you know of a definite and threatened claim that will likely lead to litigation, you should not destroy or alter any documents that may have relevance to the claims. In most cases, all you need is a "reasonable expectation" of an impending investigation of a subject area to trigger an obligation to retain all relevant documents. Failure to do so could subject you to criminal and civil penalties. For your own sake, think Enron and Arthur Andersen LLC, and that should sober you!

4. The "Back-up" Trap

Companies that have their employees' computers connected on a Local Area Network usually have procedures in place to "back-up" (save and store) everything on tape or hard drives of their servers automatically at designated intervals, such as every two days, or some other convenient period. The main servers have huge capacity hard drives and other storage devices where the e-mails (received and sent) of all employees reside until deleted.

The servers also store the database information regarding customer lists, and all other files that are part of a shared network system within your organization. Each employee who has access to that information takes it from the company's network. The "back-up" helps to protect the company and its employees from losing and having to re-create huge amounts of data if and when the system crashes, as the I.T. administrator needs only to go back to the most recent "back-up" tape to retrieve and restore the information that was on the servers as of that date.

So, how does this affect you? Quite substantially, when you unintentionally get trapped! It means that what you thought you "deleted" at any given time may not have actually been deleted, depending on your timing. It may have been "backed up" on a tape or other storage media through the company's main servers. For example, if your company backs up the e-mail system every Tuesday at 5 p.m., and you type and send an e-mail on Tuesday at 4 p.m., your e-mail will be stored that evening on the "backup" tape. Suppose you arrive at the office the next morning to delete it, having realized overnight that the e-mail you wrote contained information too sensitive to leave on your system. You open your e-mail program, highlight the message, hit "delete," and it disappears from your screen. Out of sight, maybe, but not off the record, because the message is still neatly stored, and retrievable, on the company's "back-up" tape from the night before. Your e-mail has been "trapped." If your company uses separate back-up tapes or CD-ROMs for each back-up, it could remain in archives forever. If the company uses the same back-up and keeps overwriting the old information with new and current files and messages, your e-mail message will remain there until the next back-up overwrites it.

So, if you sent an e-mail and regret what you said in it, particularly something against company policy, and you choose to delete it to avoid discovery, you may be too late to protect yourself from a backfire if you don't know how your company's "back-up" system operates. Consider what could happen when the other side delivers a subpoena that "orders" the system administrator to turn over all of the back-up tapes to the plaintiff's forensic computer expert who will create a "mirror-image" copy of them to preserve the status quo of their contents. Your untimely deletion of that unwanted e-mail keeps it stuck in the backup trap, and discoverable. At that point, all you can do is pray. Get informed now about your company's automatic backup systems, and work smarter!

5. Deleting and Deluding

Guess what? If you haven't heard enough disturbing news, here's more: Your "delete" action doesn't really delete anything. It doesn't matter whether it's an e-mail, letter, report, or spreadsheet, or blueprints, graphics, or designs. When you "delete," you delude yourself in thinking the file is gone, because with the right "abracadabra"—like magic—it can be made to reappear. The magic, though, is in the software readily available to computer technicians.

When you "delete" a file, the "delete" function simply frees up, or unlocks, space on the storage disk where the file or message originally was "saved," so future bits of data can "overwrite" the old data that still resides there. It doesn't erase the old file.

Alarmingly, the average computer user has no idea what actually happens in the deletion process! This widespread misconception in the workplace could be devastating to the company because remnants of "deleted" files, not yet overwritten, are retrievable for pre-trial discovery.

"DELETE" ERASES THE PATH TO THE FILE, NOT THE FILE ITSELF

The "delete" function erases the link to the path that leads to the file, but it never actually "deletes" the file itself. The icon on your monitor for that message folder, and the message or information contained in it, disappears from your monitor. You no longer have any pointer to get to it. But it's still on your disk drive, until it's overwritten with new data. Those remnants that haven't been overwritten are what's recovered by computer experts trained to scavenge for this untouched data.

UNDERSTANDING HOW REMNANTS ACCUMULATE ON A HARD DRIVE

When you save data (in any form, such as words, numbers, pictures, or any combination of these) your storage mechanism (hard drive, external drive, floppy disk, or CD ROM drive, it doesn't matter) simply places that data on the drive or disk and "reserves" that space until you "un-reserve" it by hitting the "delete" key. Although you see an e-mail or file as one complete unit, the operating system that makes up the brains of your computer actually sends pieces of the file or message to all different areas of the storage drive wherever it finds available space. So, your one message can actually be strewn around many different areas of the hard drive. The operating system "remembers" where these bits and pieces are stored so when you retrieve the message or file, it instantly comes up as a whole on your screen. When you click the mouse or tap a key to "delete" the file or the e-mail, the spaces that were used to place these bits and pieces of your file are freed up for other data to overwrite them, but until that happens, the bits and pieces of your data remain on the drive or disk.

The extent of how much information from these bits and pieces can be recovered depends on how much daily activity has taken place since the "deletions" occurred. The more activity, the more "overwriting" of old, reserved spaces on the drives or disks, and the less remnants there are that stay "alive," or untouched. When you "save" a future file, you have no way of directing that the bits and pieces of data from that "new" save be placed in the formerly occupied spaces to overwrite them. It all happens randomly. The more new "saves," the more chance your data will overwrite the old areas. Your operating system places the bits and pieces of data wherever there's free space—some of that space will be "clean" in the sense that no prior data was stored there, while other space will be old remnants from "deleted" files ready to be overwritten. That's why trial lawyers are being admonished to get in to your computer systems as early as they can, armed with a subpoena that authorizes it, so their experts can get a mirror copy of all of your drives before anyone has a chance to save more files, and potentially destroy the remnants that might contain some smoking "gems."

How do you get rid of these remnants?

(1) If you use the drives and have a lot of new "saves" since your old "delete" actions, there may be enough overwriting to destroy most of the old fragments.

(2) If you install new programs, they will take up a lot of storage space and likely, hit many of the old remnant areas and overwrite them. But if you do not have a lot of activity in the "save" area, much of your old "deleted" information is still in the drive and can be extracted by technicians through relatively easy methods.

(3) In the Microsoft Windows program, and in most operating systems, there is a utility program that "defragments" the drives or disks. This will help to overwrite areas of the drive by rearranging the physical location of data. It organizes your stored bits and pieces into a more compact and efficient arrangement. The defragmenting of your drive usually improves the speed of accessing information on your system because the system has an easier time pulling the pieces of a document from one area, instead of from many different areas, of the drive or disk.

(4) You can buy and use a software utility program that wipes the remnants clean from the storage areas. This "wipe" operation is similar to what happens when you record audio over the old sounds on an audio tape. Here, the "wipe" overwrites the old remnant areas of data that are no longer attached to a saved document.

Tapper's Tip #34:

To avoid the consequences that "remnants" on your hard drive can cause, your company's first course of action should be to adopt and enforce a company-wide retention policy for electronic files that tells you not only what to save, but for how long, and what you should not or need not save. The company can supplement this policy with additional approaches, including the purchase and use of software that overwrites and "erases" the remnants of those files that were deleted, and the frequent use of the "defragment" utility in the operating system.

6. The Runaway Message Trap

Once you send an e-mail you lose all control over it. You expect it to reach the person or persons to whom it's addressed, but there's no guarantee, only a potential trap as to what happens to it. If your message is confidential to persons outside your company, what do you know of their security procedures to protect its confidentiality? Who has access to the receiver's e-mails? Who is in the range of observation of the receiver's monitor when she opens the e-mail? Although some e-mail programs allow you to request a "return receipt," these same programs allow the addressee to choose not to send one. No matter, because even if you were to get one, how can you be sure that the addressee is the person who "opened" your e-mail, as opposed to someone else who may have been at the addressee's computer?

And what about the "forward pass"? How do you know the addressee won't forward your e-mail or file attachment to people you don't want it to go to? It's so easy to take an e-mail that you receive, and click on "Forward" and send it to whomever you choose. And it's equally easy to type names of people for a "forward" message, and inadvertently click your mouse before you have a chance to check the list. You may have sent the message on its speedy mission to people you didn't really want to include.

This happens more often than you'd think. Many people set up "groups" of names in their e-mail address book to streamline repeated messages to all the members of each group without having to type each name in the address line every time they send an e-mail to them. This works great in a project team, for example, or for staff members of your department. But if you're in a hurry to get an e-mail out to a few selected people, you might take a shortcut by selecting your group list, highlighting the names you want to delete from it, then clicking "send." Inadvertently, while you were doing this and handling a phone call, you deleted the wrong names and kept others who should not have been there. When confidential information is involved, it could be devastating, not only to the destruction of the "confidentiality," but to the consequences from sharing the information with the wrong people.

Although software programs are available to retrieve an e-mail before the addressee opens it, the vast majority of companies haven't purchased them. Anyone who has been around corporate offices long enough knows that when it comes to "up-to-date" computer equipment and software, companies are usually three or four generations behind the leading edge of the technology market at any given time. If your office desktop or laptop is a current market model, or within one or two generations of one, consider yourself among the "elite."

Destroying Confidentiality/Waiving Attorney-Client Privilege

The ease of forwarding an e-mail, and the lack of control over the security for its confidential handling on the receiver's end, can wreak havoc with attorney-client privileged messages. If you forward the e-mail containing legal advice from your company's attorney to anyone outside of the attorney-client relationship, you will single-handedly destroy the "privilege" of non-disclosure, and make the e-mail message discoverable by a future plaintiff. This means that when the plaintiff's attorney demands to see all communications on your computer as part of normal pre-trial discovery, the company's attorneys have no defense to shield that communication from disclosure. They'll have to produce the message, even if it has potentially damaging information. And when they do, someone from an executive office will be yelling the familiar refrain of sports fans, "Who let the dogs out?" When you hear it, start kissing your upcoming promotion good-bye.

Tapper's Tip #35:

Never forward an e-mail message (or an attachment to it) when it's from an attorney addressed to you, no matter whether the attorney is from in-house or outside, without first getting the permission from the attorney to do so. Even if the message is your own, addressed to the attorney, and you desire to forward a copy of it to someone else, do not do so unless you consult with the attorney in advance. Once you have disclosed the message to someone outside the circle of people who have a "right" to know, or a "need to know," within the circle of "client" status, you destroy the privilege.

Tapper's Tip #36:

Label your e-mail message in the subject line with "Attorney-Client Privileged Communication" and "Confidential" to alert the recipient to give it special handling. It will also help you when searching your e-mails at a later date to clean out your archives, so you can treat these differently and find them more easily.

7. The Date-Time Tattoo Trap

The automatic date and time stamping feature of e-mails is both a "positive" and a "negative" as a communication tool. Every e-mail you send bears the sender's name, the recipient's name, and a "fingerprint," which is the actual date and time the message was sent. If your e-mail program has the return-receipt feature for e-mails you send, the receipt will show the time and date the recipient opened the message (unless, of course, she chooses not to send you one).

The "fingerprint" data for the e-mails that you send from your PC may not be reliable. The date and time is dependent on the internal clock setting in your PC. If you haven't paid attention to its accuracy (for example, each person has the option of setting the internal clock for regional time zones, daylight savings, and A.M. and P.M.), the "record" you create by the imprint on an e-mail as to date and time will forever suffer from this infirmity. At a future time, which could be years later, this e-mail could become a central piece of evidence in litigation (you never know if it will, for it usually happens when you least expect it). You may be dumbfounded by then if the time of the e-mail doesn't synchronize with your own recollection from diary entries in your old office planner.

How will you prove your computer's clock was inaccurate at the time you sent an e-mail, after years have passed since the e-mail was written? Your original PC or its internal configuration may no longer exist, having been replaced a few times, or upgraded internally. Suppose the issue in litigation centers on when your company sent an e-mail notice of cancellation of a purchase order. The vendor argues the notice was too late; it already incurred expenses in filling the order. The timing of your cancellation is crucial for the defense. It's an uphill battle, though, if you have to discredit the time stamp on the e-mail. People tend to believe what they see in writing, especially when the paper version of the e-mail, enlarged to a 3 ft. by 4 ft. foam board, sits on an easel in front of a jury.

Tapper's Tip #37:

Consult the manual for your PC's or Mac's operating system to be sure you understand how to set the internal clock. Make the effort to periodically check on its accuracy.

8. The Interception Trap

Some people use a Web-based e-mail system to check their e-mails when on the road. Web-based e-mail systems provide free e-mail accounts to anyone with access to the Internet. When you sign up for this free service (which may not remain "free" for long, as these services are now looking for ways to charge a user), you can choose your own e-mail address provided it's not the same as, or similar to, others already taken. Your clients or customers can use that address to send messages to you when they know you're on the road, or you can have your office messages forwarded to a web-based site without a client ever knowing they're forwarded. Or, you can simply retrieve the messages from your company's network, as always, by using a remote access code.

If you use the web-based public site, your e-mails lose the security they otherwise would have on a closed company network, because your e-mails will then reside on a server not owned or controlled by anyone in your company. You have no way of knowing who sees them or has access to them at the company that hosts the site.

Even companies with a closed network and a private intra-company e-mail system must engage an Internet Service Provider to connect to the World Wide Web if they expect employees to send e-mails to people outside the company. Those e-mails travel by relay from public server to public server until they reach the people addressed.

If the person addressed has an e-mail account with a public e-mail host, such as America Online® or Earthlink®, the e-mail is stored on their servers around the world, depending on where the sender and receiver are located. It is no more secure if the person to whom you're addressing the e-mail is inside a company that has its own private network, similar to your company's. That's because although the message will be stored on his company's main server, it very likely was routed through an Internet Service Provider whose public servers relayed your message to him.

The problem is you don't know who in those public or private e-mail host systems has access to those e-mails. You just don't know what security procedures, if any, are in place at these locations, and how effectively they're enforced. Can you be sure that appropriate precautions have been taken there to prevent snooping by unauthorized persons? Consider what would happen if either the public host or the company that received your e-mail is subpoenaed by a government agency to turn over its e-mail logs, and your e-mails are sitting on either system.

And don't forget the paper trail you might leave if you make a diary entry in your calendar or planner that mentions you e-mailed someone outside your company on a particular date. Your e-mail may still be discovered even if you deleted it from your computer; the opposing attorney will simply serve a subpoena on the person you mentioned in your diary and demand a copy of it from her computer. The solution? Be careful of your notations in planners, and only send e-mail content outside your company if it can withstand public disclosure.

HERE ARE SOME ADDITIONAL THINGS YOU SHOULD BE AWARE OF TO AVOID THE "INTERCEPTION TRAP":

Hackers

Hackers generally have an easier time of accessing e-mails on public web servers, compared to accessing e-mails on a company's private servers. The information you send in your e-mail message or file attachment is broken into bits of data to pass more efficiently through cyberspace. These bits of data are sent through routers, from one location to the other, until they reach their destination. With the right equipment and technical know-how, a person hired by, or working for a competitor, or someone with criminal intent, is capable of checking for certain bits of data as they pass through these routers. By having access to any server where the mail is temporarily stored, or to the system where your receiver's mail is delivered, a hacker can play havoc with your message, downloading it, reading it, or even modifying it. Also, software programs that have voice-mail and answering machine functions, or fax capabilities through a modem, provide additional vulnerability to hackers because these programs work with passwords for access. Hackers have programs that run algorithms on the infinite varieties of passwords to capture yours, and gain entry into your system.

Firewalls

The degree of difficulty for an outsider to penetrate the security of your company's e-mail system depends on how strong a "firewall" the company has installed to protect the system. The firewall is a software program, sometimes combined with hardware accessories, that builds protection around a company's computer files to resist an outsider's entry, without permission. These programs vary, as do the degrees of protection, but they're readily available on the market.

Encryption

Another way you can help protect against hackers breaking into your e-mails is through encryption. A program with encryption functions takes your e-mail message or file attachment and translates it into a code that only the receiver can decipher through a program at the receiver's end that recognizes the code. There are, also, a number of reputable third-party vendors who provide secure encryption services for your Website, assisting your customers in making purchases by credit card. You know their system is operating when you see the little yellow padlock at the bottom of your monitor, signifying the information you're sending is encrypted.

Encryption programs are essential if you intend to send confidential information in your e-mail, either as part of the text, or as an attached file.

Theft and Misappropriation

The ease of attaching files of any kind to e-mails makes your company especially vulnerable to theft and misappropriation of trade secrets and other proprietary information. How easy it is for disgruntled employees, who can sense their impending termination, to "click and send" customer lists, and other sensitive information, to competitors, or to their home PC's and their personal e-mail accounts where they store it for future access. (Chapter 7 addresses this major concern for companies in high tech businesses, as well as those in the retail and service-dominated industries.)

9. The Snooping Eyes Trap

Confidentiality requires secrecy, a restricted audience, and attention for special handling. To live up to the requirements of maintaining confidentiality in the e-mail environment, consider the potential accessibility, or "snooper" potential, of your PC.

> ### Tapper's Tip #38:
>
> If you can open your PC's operating system and start working without need of a password, you're looking for trouble. Set up your operating system, in addition to your e-mail program, with unique passwords, so only *you* can access your files and messages.

Access to your PC should be restricted to your eyes only, either through a password or a key lock. In addition to passwording your entire system (where boot-up won't occur until you enter the correct password), you can protect access to important files (not just e-mails) by "locking" them each with a password. It's an easy procedure, but one that's all too often ignored.

What about your system administrator? Can people in Information Technology override your password, and gain access to your files? If so, high level confidentiality will be compromised, especially if you're an attorney, or the client, and have sent or received an attorney-client privileged communication.

> ### Tapper's Tip #39:
>
> Don't let anyone sit at your PC without monitoring the activity, even for a moment. When you're not looking, a damaging or embarrassing e-mail can be sent, in an instant, from your PC to other people, and your e-mail address will be the source. This may start as a prank, but turn ugly for you real soon.

Consider what could happen if others can access your PC. You could be "set up" by somebody, and I'm not being paranoid. All you need is a disgruntled co-worker who wants some revenge, especially if you're on a managerial level. People can send disparaging e-mails with racist comments, or ones branding you for a sexual discrimination claim, all from your PC, and make it look as if they came from you. The e-mail could be sent to a colleague, to your boss, or to an outsider. What are you and your company doing to guard against it?

Tapper's Tip #40:

How you position your desktop monitor can mean the difference between breaching the confidentiality of a document, or securing it. If your office is situated in a manner that makes your monitor visible to incoming visitors, you need extra vigilance when viewing, or typing, confidential material.

Here's where the "snoop" factor comes in. If your back is toward your office door when working at your desktop PC, you may not be aware of someone standing in the doorway as you're typing a confidential memo. Avoid the potential of someone studying your monitor while you are unaware of his presence. When possible, reposition the monitor so you face the door when working at your desktop.

Tapper's Tip #41:

If the layout of your office does not lend itself to re-positioning your monitor's screen, consider buying a small, round, convex mirror (about 2"in diameter), sold at auto stores. Its original purpose is to eliminate rear view "blind spots" on exterior car door mirrors. But it can help you when you're not driving, too. If you stick one on the front, top corner of your monitor cabinet, with the self-stick adhesive tape it comes with, you'll always see who's behind you while you're working at your PC. You'll have your own rear-view mirror.

And one more precaution to take against a snooper's eyes: Never leave your desk while your computer system is open to your e-mails. Typically, after a short period of time, your monitor goes into "sleep" mode and your screen saver will come on. All it takes to "wake-up" the monitor is a bump on the mouse. If someone comes in to your office to put a paper on your desk, and happens to give the slightest bump to your keyboard drawer or mouse, the screen saver will vanish, and your e-mail screen will appear in all its bright and readable glory. Not the best of circumstances, if your e-mails have confidential information in them.

Tapper's Tip #42:

Always close-out your e-mail program if you leave your desk or office area, even if it's to go the restroom, break room, or copy station. That way, your e-mails are protected from the "snooper," as they can only be read by entering your password, and opening the program again.

The "Other" Breeding Grounds

Beyond E-mails and E-files

Although e-mails and electronic files give us enough fertile ground for smoking guns, the things you do to conduct your business, whether in the workplace or on the road, are breeding grounds for so many more—like holding confidential discussions on a cell phone, writing "incident" reports that backfire, exaggerating employee performance evaluations, posting cartoons or jokes on a bulletin board, hanging decorations on office walls and cabinets, using laptop computers without securing the information in them, and talking too much, giving away inside information unintentionally. This is just a sampling.

You run into situations everyday that are prone to producing smoking guns. I'll introduce you to 17 of them in this chapter, by necessity the largest in the book. To assist you in our journey, I've divided it into four parts.

In Part One—*Communications*—you'll be surprised at how easy it is for you and your colleagues to inadvertently produce smoking guns by simply talking, faxing, or using a laptop.

Part Two—*Risk Management*—gives you money-saving suggestions for your company that can actually be worth millions if implemented. When a company stops committing the kinds of blunders I reveal, it can stand up and face its opposition with confidence and strength.

In Part Three—*Employment*—I'll alert you to four situations and show you how to protect yourself and your company in future employment-related claims and lawsuits.

Part Four—*Infrastructure*—is for those who are in companies that do business through subsidiaries. I'll show you how a relatively common situation in the relationship between a parent company and its subsidiary corporations can leave the parent company "holding the bag" for the acts of its subsidiaries, a result that's just the opposite of what the parent wants.

As I take you through these breeding grounds, I suspect that more than once, you'll say, "I didn't realize that," or, "I never thought of that." Don't worry, it's a normal reaction. It simply underscores the fact that, most of the time, employees don't intentionally create smoking guns. They stumble into them. By the time we finish our journey, though, you, at least, should stumble no more.

Through guidance and awareness, you CAN protect yourself and the company from words and actions that backfire.

Here's our guide of the breeding grounds we'll cover in each Part:

PART ONE: COMMUNICATIONS

1-1. Cell Phone Talk: *Can you hear me?*

1-2. Voice-Mails: *Let's keep it confidential...NOT!*

1-3. Faxes: *Who's on the other end?*

1-4. Talking to Strangers: *Remembering what Mom told you.*

1-5. Trade Show Talk: *"I'm talking ...and I can't shut up!"*

1-6. Laptop On the Road: *Are the company's secrets "in good hands"?*

PART TWO: RISK MANAGEMENT

2-1. Incident Reports: *Facts...only the facts...but which ones?*

2-2. Surveillance Videos: *Candid camera works both ways.*

2-3. Evidence: *Chain of custody—who will be the weakest link?*

2-4. Hiring an Expert: *Gem or surprise package?*

2-5. The Company "On Notice": *Knock, knock...is anybody there?*

2-6. Laptops and Desktops Discarded: *Junkyard dogs or bounty of gold?*

PART THREE: EMPLOYMENT

3-1. Web Bulletin Boards: *Who's watching?*

3-2. Physical Surroundings: *Look and ye shall offend.*

3-3. Performance Evaluations: *Straighten up and fly right.*

3-4. Background Checks: *Flushing out the weeds.*

PART FOUR: INFRASTRUCTURE

4-1. Parent/Subsidiary Relations: *Love me or leave me?*

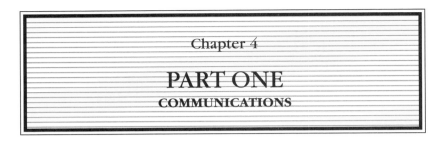

1-1. Cell Phone Talk: *Can you hear me?*

There's hardly a place you can go without seeing someone talking on a cell phone. Despite advances from analog to digital technology, security from interception of your conversations is still not trustworthy enough to risk discussing important information you want to keep confidential.

> ### Tapper's Tip #43
>
> As a rule, when you talk to anyone on a cell phone (no matter if both parties are using cells, or just one party), you should not discuss confidential or privileged information.

That not only holds true for business talk, but for personal conversations, too. The chances are too great that your call can be intercepted, or crossed with another mobile phone line, without your knowing it. It happened to me one morning while driving to my office. I made a few cell phone calls to get a head start for the day. What a surprise when one of my colleagues, who was driving the same route to the office as I was at the time, revealed later that he heard my conversation as he was talking on his cell phone to someone else. The lines, somehow, got crossed. Luckily, the discussion wasn't confidential. It was a wake-up call, though. This isn't the medium to carry on a conversation if you want it to be confidential.

Aside from interception, think about the people who can overhear your end of the conversation simply by being near you while you engage in the call, and you know that most of the time you're not in a secure environment while talking. After all, cell phones are for convenience, not security, and you can easily forget the different consequences of "public" conversations.

Did you ever attend a business convention or seminar and observe what happens at break time? Everybody makes a mad dash to the phones to check in with the office or listen to voicemails. They'll use the bank of pay phones in the lobbies or walk 'n talk their way to the restrooms with cell phones at their ears. Can you not help overhearing their conversations in such close proximity in the lounge and refreshment areas?

What about the volume of your cell phone speaking voice? I don't know about you, but I know that when I'm surrounded by a lot of noise—whether it's in an airplane with the drone of jet engines, or in a crowded area with the sounds of other people talking—I have a tendency to speak louder into the cell phone to help hear myself better, even though it makes my conversation easier to be overheard. Like everyone else, I tend to think that if there's a lot of noise around me, no one else will hear my conversation.

Tapper's Tip #44

Be more diligent next time you use your cell phone—or any other phone—in public. Consider who might be overhearing your conversation. If there's anything confidential about it, try this: Think of the person next to you as either a lawyer who has a case pending against your company, or an employee of a competitor, taking notes on what you're saying.

The person in your vicinity could be one of thousands of employees in your company who recognizes you, although you don't know her. If she misinterprets what she hears from your side of the cell phone conversation and repeats it to her co-workers, and they, in turn, tell it to others, the life-cycle of a rumor begins its course.

Now assume you were talking to your company's attorney on the cell phone and the conversation took place while you were waiting for your meal in a crowded restaurant where the tables were close together. Months later, you've been called to give a deposition and the topic of your restaurant conversation just so happens to be relevant to the issues in the litigation. The opposing attorney asks you about that conversation, but your company's attorney immediately objects, and directs you not to answer on the ground that it was an attorney-client privileged communication.

The opposing attorney is allowed to probe the issue of whether the conversation qualifies as "privileged." He asks you about the details of where, when, and how your conversation took place, and who was present within hearing distance. If you allowed others to overhear your end of the conversation and they were not part of the attorney-client relationship, you may have unwittingly destroyed the privilege of non-disclosure. The consequence: You're required to reveal the substance and content of the entire conversation to the opposing attorney!

Tapper's Tip #45

Always be circumspect in your conversations involving business, and never indulge in such conversation in close surroundings, particularly in restaurants, lunch rooms, or in airplanes, as you never know who is overhearing you at the next table, booth, or seat behind you.

And don't think that just because your cell phone conversation is with the company's attorney who is engaging you in the discussion, that makes everything okay. It doesn't. I can't tell you how many times I had to stop discussions on a cell phone with another attorney when I considered the information as "confidential," even though the other attorney was willing to keep talking. I would always postpone the discussion until we could get to a "land" line, which was more secure.

Tapper's Tip #46

Be vigilant, and don't rely on others—even if they're the company's attorneys—to decide if it's all right to talk confidentially on a cell phone. Save all confidential discussions for secure environments.

1-2. Voice-Mails: *Let's keep it confidential...NOT!*

Large companies usually have an administrator in charge of telecommunication facilities, and passwords are assigned to, or chosen by, employees for private access to their voice-mail box. Accepting the "default," or common password configuration (such as your first name's initial with three letters of your last name, or a number combination that's your home address or birth date), is unwise because other employees (and sometimes their friends) also know the default pattern. That can lead to unauthorized, and undetected, access of your voice-mails.

Most of the time the system administrator has the ability to override your password and play the recordings that have accumulated in your voice-mail box. They're usually not supposed to access your voice mail without your permission, as a matter of company policy and ethics, but the opportunity is always there, and it's difficult to detect if it happens.

Tapper's Tip #47

If your in-house counsel uses a voice-mail system that's accessible by an administrator, the privileged status of an attorney-client confidential message on the system may become vulnerable. An aggressive trial lawyer can mount a formidable challenge to "bust" the non-disclosure protection by showing how employees who are not part of the "client" relationship have access to the message.

It's a question of security, and the measures and procedures the law department has established, to protect its communications.

Tapper's Tip #48

Never leave confidential information on anyone's voice mail, unless you're not concerned about destroying its confidentiality. Better to leave a message that only tells the recipient to call you back because you have some confidential information you want to share. Human curiosity, with a little intrigue, usually provokes a prompt call-back.

You don't know if the message you leave is being recorded on an internal system where the playback can only be heard by the person assigned to that voice mail-box when she calls in with her passcode, or on an external answering machine (like the kind most people have at home) that records or plays back your message out loud from a built-in speaker. If all someone has to do is hit the right button to play back the messages on an external table-top machine, or pass by someone's office and overhear a message as it's coming in and being recorded, there's no such thing as a "confidential" voice-mail.

1-3. Faxes: *Who's on the other end?*

When you communicate by fax, you face two significant risks: breaching the confidentiality of the information, and delivering it to the wrong person.

These risks are inherent in the nature of the fax machine setup in most offices. If the fax machine sits in a workroom or copy center where it's in operation almost continually, someone has to sort the incoming faxes, or spread them on a table, until secretaries or executives come looking for their names on the fax cover sheets to pick them out of the assortment throughout the day. It's a buffet table, with faxes as the serving.

If you have this arrangement, there can be no confidentiality because anyone with access to the center can view them. No matter that they have a "cover" sheet. Anyone can still lift it up, flip the page, and see the document underneath. And how many times has someone in the fax center made an error by stapling a cover sheet to the wrong document? When you know this has happened more than once, while waiting for an important fax you thought you never received, you start to mistrust the competency of whoever is assembling the faxes. You begin looking at the faxed pages themselves, instead of relying on the cover sheets. And in the process, you're seeing everyone else's fax documents. Some day, an attorney will have a rude awakening when an opposing attorney challenges the privileged status of a document that has been sent to a company via fax, and its fax machine is part of an internal copy center where numerous people have access to the faxes.

Tapper's Tip #49

When you're sending a fax to an attorney in an attorney-client relationship (or, if the attorney is sending one to you), the nature of the fax machine setup on either side can make a difference in whether the communication will be protected from disclosure in future litigation.

In another type of arrangement, one person might be "in charge" of the fax-receiving area. That person will sort the faxes and deliver them to the appropriate recipients by personal delivery, or through the company's mail distribution system. Since the faxes are still open and visible, the security for protecting confidential information is no better than sending the information through the mail via postcard. Unless the faxes are enclosed in a separate, sealed envelope, you really have no security for their confidential content.

As to the sending of a fax, despite the red flag you put on the cover sheet that says "Confidential," if it's addressed to the wrong person, or to the right person with the wrong fax number, you have destroyed confidentiality, and risk having the document fall into the wrong hands.

Speed-dialing systems add to that potential hazard. They enable you to program fax numbers by using a single number as a reference code. By hitting one number, the fax machine automatically dials the full number of the addressee assigned to the speed-dial code. How easy it is, in an afternoon of backed-up faxes and frazzled employees, to send a document to the wrong party by hitting the wrong speed-dial code. What if that document had all the deal terms of an anticipated new business acquisition that's highly confidential, particularly for a publicly-traded company, subject to insider trading regulations? Sometimes, the speed-dial system can be programmed to send a fax to a multitude of addressees by hitting one speed code number for a group. Imagine the havoc that could cause for you when the wrong code gets punched! Then again, who wants to even think of that nightmare?

Tapper's Tip #50

If you're sending a confidential fax that should only be seen by the eyes of the addressee, always call the addressee, beforehand, to arrange for her to stand by her fax machine to receive your fax as it goes through. Request that you be called back to confirm its personal receipt. To do otherwise is to destroy confidentiality and, in an attorney-client privileged document, risk the loss of its protected status.

Tapper's Tip #51

If most of the information you deal with is confidential, and sending or receiving it by fax is the most convenient for you, install a fax machine, dedicated to your exclusive use, in your own personal office, to assure privacy.

1-4. Talking to Strangers:
Remembering what mom told you.

TELEPHONE INQUIRIES

It's astonishing to learn how much information strangers can get from company receptionists or employees in specific departments just by calling and introducing themselves. Experts in the corporate intelligence-gathering business tell how easy it is to get proprietary information from ordinary people at all kinds of companies, big and small. With the right questions and techniques, callers and visiting sales people have been able to get the dollar amounts of daily and weekly sales, types of sales, a list of best-selling products, information on new product developments, and more.

Tapper's Tip #52

Your employees should be trained in what to say to strangers who call and inquire about details of your company, including its internal structure, products, sales activities, and financial data. Restrict the kinds of information given over the phone by referring callers to the company's Web site, or by offering a brochure in the mail.

Your company's representative should refrain from readily offering any such information and should request that the caller mail or fax a letter, on letterhead, to your company formally requesting the information he wants. This will enable you to check out the legitimacy of the caller with appropriate authorities and sources.

I'm not referring to customer service inquiries that relate to real problems with your products or services, as they should be dealt with promptly and effectively. The suspicious inquiries are those that ask probing questions about your company, its officers, their functions, your products, etc. These queries are unrelated to solving a customer's experience with your product or service.

Also beware of private firms that provide reference check services for former employees who want to know what previous employers are saying about them. For a fee, the company will "pose" as an employer who has your former employee under consideration as a candidate for a job, and ask you a number of questions about your opinion of the person's past job performance and traits. Their only purpose is to report back to the former employee everything you said. They'll also serve as a witness to the conversation, if needed, should the former employee decide to sue you or your company for slander, or an action called "interfering with an economic opportunity" (such as getting another job).

Tapper's Tip #53

Train your staff to refer all inquiries about former employees to a central location, preferably the Human Resource department, where the company policy is to give no information by phone.

They should respond only to written inquiries that require no more than verification of employment dates, titles, and prior job functions. To be sure, though, you should check with your company's counsel just in case you are in a state that has laws that require employers to give any more information than that, depending on who's asking for it.

ON-PREMISES INQUIRIES

More often than you'd think, in companies with retail establishments, where customers have the opportunity to mingle with front-line employees, an attorney representing a person who has either filed suit against your company or is getting ready to, will enter your premises as a "customer." The front-line employees are the ones who are visible and readily available to the public. They include department store clerks, sales people, customer service representatives, shipping department employees, delivery personnel, bellhops, security persons, cashiers, maintenance workers, front desk clerks, valet parkers, casino change attendants, and housekeeping personnel.

She'll engage your employee in customer-friendly banter, which can turn to more pointed questions like: "Have you ever seen anyone fall over there [name an area of the property]?" "How many have you seen?" "What do you think made them fall?" "Has anybody told management about these conditions?" "Do you think management cares about it?" "What has management done about it so far?" The employees, believing it's good customer service to be friendly, innocently voice their opinions and inside knowledge, not realizing the damage they do to themselves and the company.

If it's "good stuff" the attorney is hearing (translate: negative smoking gun-type talk about how lax the management is, and how nobody follows-up on complaints in-house), you can bet that employee has talked himself onto a list of depositions the attorney will want to take. The attorney will need to get the employee "on record."

And if, by the time of his deposition, the employee has changed his responses from those he originally gave, a good trial lawyer will probe into the reason. She'll want to know whom the employee has talked to since their original meeting, whether management admonished him not to talk, and whether anyone "refreshed his recollection" about how events actually happened. If managers did have a "closed door" conversation with the employee about the potential damage of his words, those managers will be next on the list of upcoming depositions. Depending on what was said in those "heart-to-heart" talks--all of which are fair game for discovery--the die is cast for a backfire.

So, take heed: Better to have trained your employees, in advance, about the danger of talking to "inquiring strangers," than to reap the consequences of their unenlightened conversations.

In many states, attorneys who have clients suing your company are not permitted to question current employees of the company without the knowledge and permission of your company's counsel. To ignore that is an ethics violation that could result in disciplinary proceedings by a state licensing authority. Some states, however, don't follow that rule, and allow attorneys to contact non-management employees for "limited" questioning, without advance notice to the company's counsel. When this occurs, it denies in-house counsel or the company's outside counsel the opportunity to meet with employees, in advance of any questioning, to advise them of the nature of the claim, and how the things they say can backfire on them. The rationale behind the "limited" questioning rule is that non-management employees' opinions are considered "personal," and not binding on the company in a "representative" capacity, so they can do no harm to the company's defense.

That all may sound logical in theory, but it ignores reality. Jurors can be prejudiced by what they hear a front-line employee say about the company because he's a person "on the inside." You can tell jurors all you want about how the employee didn't represent management's opinion, but what he said will still have a psychological effect on them. Trial lawyers know that. All they need is for the bell to ring; after that, you can't "un-ring" it.

So, how do you control this? Through training, training, and more training! You need to hold workshops for your employees where you effectively drive home the importance of not talking to "customers" or other outsiders about specific risk management topics. Show them why such information is "confidential," and how, by giving it to these people, they will involve themselves in the pending litigation (which will take time away from their jobs when they're called for depositions, and most probably, appearances in court at trial time).

Tapper's Tip #54

Train your employees—and make it a directive—to give no information to outsiders who approach them with questions unrelated to current customer service requests. Direct them to treat all questioners that probe for information about the company, or anything that has happened at the company, with suspicion. Have them always ask for a business card which should, then, be referred to in-house counsel or a member of upper management.

Company directives should require that any time employees get inquiries of a "risk management" nature (defining this will be part of the training), the first thing they should ask the person is, "Are you an attorney?" Attorneys who misrepresent that answer are subject to professional discipline in the state in which they are licensed. Sometimes, the person may be a private investigator hired by an attorney. In either event, your employee should demand a business card before saying anything further. After that, the inquirer should be told that questions of the type being asked are reserved for management, and a company person's name and phone number should be given for contact. (If you have an in-house lawyer in your establishment, the employee should call the company's lawyer immediately to advise of the person on the premises.)

If your company establishes a corporate culture where, as part of the job functions of every employee, participation in proactive risk management activities and procedures is expected, employees will feel a responsibility for mishaps that occur to customers. Most of the risk management blunders in a company happen because of inattentiveness of employees. They either do not perform their jobs as diligently as they should, or see something that could be a hazard, but do nothing about it, because of an "It's not my job" attitude.

Tapper's Tip #55

Risk management is EVERYBODY's job in the workplace, and there should be no exceptions, right up to the executive boardroom.

With effective programs and training that includes *all* employees, your company can save at least 25 percent (and in many cases, much more) of its current risk management liability costs (which include costs of claims and defense of litigation). I know it can be done because I've done it.

1-5. Trade Show Talk:
"I'm talking...and I can't shut up!"

Want to learn all about the inner workings of a company, and all of its inside scuttlebutt? Just spend some time showing interest in the company's products and processes at its trade booth at the next major convention. Pose as a "novice" in the industry and ask a lot of questions. Corporate intelligence firms report that it's one of the easiest places to gather competitor's inside information; sales reps who tend the booth are eager to talk.

Tapper's Tip #56

To protect your company against inadvertently giving out confidential information at places like trade shows, conventions, and sales presentations, your salespeople must be trained, beforehand, in the difference between generally available vs. proprietary information. It's the company's job to identify for them what is "proprietary," or of "trade secret" status.

Too often, it's not the salespeople's fault—they're just not informed accurately, in layman's language, by the company's legal staff. Descriptions of proprietary information are usually given in vague references rather than specifics. To be sure, the company itself often has not taken the time to inventory its trade secrets and other proprietary information to the point where it can identify specifics, instead of generalities. Take inventory now!

Tapper's Tip #57

If your company is serious about protecting its information, it should invest in a full-blown audit of intellectual property, including trade secrets and other proprietary information. You need to know what your company has in its archives and current database before you can adequately instruct employees on what **not** to talk about.

1-6. Laptop On the Road:
Are the company's secrets "in good hands"?

PHYSICAL SECURITY:

Laptop computers are easy targets for thieves who see an attractive resale value on the "hot" market. At least 70% of Fortune 1000 companies have experienced laptop thefts. Although it's bad enough losing your laptop, it's even worse knowing you've compromised highly confidential information about your company (and maybe your personal life, too) by storing it on the hard drive, or leaving it on a disk or CD ROM, inside the computer.

Tapper's Tip #58

When you carry your company's laptop, you have a responsibility to protect it from theft. Treat it the same as you would your wallet.

Laptop thievery doesn't discriminate. It happened at the offices of the Federal Bureau of Investigation where over a hundred laptops were missing or unaccounted for in July, 2001. Some of them contained highly sensitive information. It also happened at what is supposed to be one of the country's most highly secure nuclear laboratories, the Los Alamos facility, where hard drives containing nuclear missile codes were missing, and eventually found, behind a copy machine. It happened, as well, at a major hotel, where the CEO of one of the nation's leading companies in wireless technology walked away from the podium for fifteen minutes in a meeting room where he had just used his laptop in a presentation to a group of business people. On his return, he discovered that someone had stolen his laptop containing what was reported as highly secretive and proprietary information about the company and its technology.

Although securing the laptop in the workplace is a basic, and essential, precaution with readily available tie-down locks, security precautions are most needed on the road. Most of those thefts occur in the airport, at the metal detector stations, where thieves work quickly in a crowd amidst confusion as your belongings make their way through the x-ray conveyor belts, mixed with other people's carry-ons. Your laptop is also an easy target in a hotel room, when it sits invitingly on a table or desk.

Aside from theft, losses occur just as frequently from a user's lax handling and inattentiveness. In New York City, alone, over 2900 laptops were left behind in taxi cabs in the year 2000!

INFORMATION SECURITY

If you're on the road, and you must carry files containing trade secrets or other proprietary and confidential information, you'd be better off storing the information on a CD ROM than on the laptop's hard drive. You can protect the information by password-protecting it, making access more difficult for intruders. Once the information is on portable disks or a CD ROM , keep these in a briefcase, satchel, or handbag, separate from your laptop.

Tapper's Tip #59

Don't store confidential information on your laptop's hard drive. Keep it on portable storage media, such as CD ROMs or floppy disks, and keep them in your possession at all times, separate from your laptop.

Another alternative is to purchase encryption software that protects the information on the hard drive with special password "keys" that make the information irretrievable without a special "key" code to "unlock" it. (If you travel internationally, though, you should check with your company's counsel, because some countries forbid entry of encrypted products.) Products are now available to "lock" a system's information and unlock it through biometric validation that requires a scan of your thumbprint. If you insist on putting highly secretive data on your laptop's hard drive, prudence dictates that you not leave your office without these added security protections.

Guard the information you carry for the worth it has to your company, realizing the value it would give to your company's competitors. Trade secrets (including customer lists), and new research and development projects, rank among the most valuable assets your company owns. When you take any of that information on the road, you assume a significant responsibility and burden to protect it. As an executive officer of your company, your negligence could expose you to a class action shareholders' suit for breach of your fiduciary duty to protect the company's assets. It may all depend on how valuable the trade secret is to the company's lifeblood. Why chance its loss?

Visibility:

How many of you have traveled to your destination by air, and sat next to a business person who worked on her laptop during the flight? You try not to look at the laptop's screen, but the seats are so close, it's awkward to avoid it. Curiosity gets the best of us, so you glance over every so often. After all, you're bored silly, aren't you? On passengers' laptops I've seen company sales projections for the next quarter, sales results by region for the past year, and a company's financial objectives on a Powerpoint presentation, together with the new project development initiatives on the drawing boards. I've also seen correspondence, as it was being typed on the laptop's keyboard, about new deals in progress. How's that for maintaining confidentiality?

When you combine this with lots of friendly conversation with your seatmate about where you work, what you do, and all kinds of details about your company that you're willing to share, the combination is powerful. I'm always amazed at seeing this blatant breach of confidentiality of proprietary information by employees (high ranking ones, particularly) and wonder if they realize what they're doing, or if they've ever been trained about confidentiality in the workplace?

Tapper's Tip #60

Think twice before opening your laptop for business in any environment where others can oversee your work. Remember your ethical and legal obligation to protect the confidentiality of company secrets and inside information, not generally available to the public. Don't compromise it for the sake of your convenience, and don't ever let your guard down.

Chapter 4

PART TWO
RISK MANAGEMENT

2-1. Incident Reports:
The facts, m'am...only the facts—but which ones?

Companies with traditional retail or service operations have their share of personal injury incidents involving their customers or guests. When a patron is injured, from whatever cause, the details of what, when, where, and how it happened are usually recorded on an "incident" or "accident" report which becomes part of the business records of the company. The incident report is discoverable, and has to be produced to the other side when the injured patron sues your company and alleges the injury was the company's fault through the action or inaction of your employees.

Tapper's Tip #61

The incident report is the most significant record of the potential claim by the customer against your company, and could be a powerful tool in building your defense position. Learn to use it wisely. Make it fortify, not mortify.

Yet, the subject of how to complete the report to gain the most advantage for the company's best interest usually receives little, or inadequate, attention. If your company has its own security force on duty, it may have assigned to certain of its members the responsibility for investigating incidents and completing the report. Security personnel today are drawn, in large part, from the ranks of retired police officers. They're used to filling out police reports as a bureaucratic formality, and still remember the tedium of it all.

In the private sector, however, the report should be considered as much more than just "another form." Approaching the report from a defense litigation viewpoint, you can make it a valuable tool for defending your company. But it requires a combination of good training and motivated employees who are eager to move beyond "filling out" a form. To ignore this is to risk having your own business records come back to haunt you.

Tapper's Tip #62

There's a lot of power in the information your employees collect and how they write it on a properly drafted form. What your employees write in the report can either "do you well" or "do you in."

I'm not talking about falsehoods here. This is a situation where true, objective details, keenly observed, make a huge difference. On a slip and fall incident, for example, observing the condition of the shoes a person is wearing, and whether that person is wearing eyeglasses and if so, how strong a prescription (by observing the thickness of the lenses) can provide beneficial details that can help the defense.

One of the most popular workshops I conduct at companies is on the topic of "Bullet-proofing Your Incident Report: Making It Work For *You*, Not Your Opponent!" It's an area that can literally save millions of dollars of potential liability for companies. Here are examples of two very significant areas where your employees' untrained words or actions could backfire:

Example #1) **Photographing the injury or scene.**

In most cases, it's unwise to photograph the customer who has been injured. Those retail chains that have a policy of not doing so have a good reason: A photo usually distorts the claim in favor of the injured party.

For example, if a customer cuts her finger on a sharp piece of shelving material while picking an item from a shelf, by the time your employee arrives to take a picture there could be blood running down and dripping from the customer's arm, making it look as if there's a major, gruesome injury. Yet, after cleaning it up, the injury reveals itself as a small surface cut about a half-inch in length, the kind that's nicely covered by a child-size, adhesive bandage, from a first aid kit.

Once you take the "bloody" photograph, it's part of the file, which is discoverable and usable by the plaintiff's lawyer. It will provide a huge emotional advantage for the plaintiff's lawyer who wants the jury to gasp and sense the "pain" from this "gruesome" injury, even though the photo misrepresents the true nature of the cut.

Tapper's Tip #63

There's no law that I know of that requires any company to photograph an injured patron. So why do so for the benefit of your adversary's lawyer? *You* should be the one to gain the advantage...before the other side takes it!

Another instance where photography works against the company is with an inexperienced employee who arrives, after the fact, at a first-aid station to interview an injured customer who fell a few moments earlier. He asks the injured party where she fell, to which the response is, "somewhere on the parking lot near a light pole." Your employee then wants to impress management with a "complete" report, so he takes his trusty camera on a photo safari. He looks around, sees some poles, then searches the area to see if there's anything the lady might have slipped or tripped on, *in his view.*

Although the injured person never mentioned slipping on any substance, the employee sees an oil spot in a parking space near "a light pole." "Aha!" he says. So, he takes a picture of the oil spot, and makes sure to angle it so the light pole is in clear view. The photo gets attached to the file and, in later discovery, produced to the plaintiff's lawyer. She shows it to her client, who then "remembers" that something made her "slip," and the client points to the oil puddle as the likely cause of her fall. The photo has served as a suggestive stimulus for the injured party.

Your employee's good intentions served the plaintiff well, but did you no good. Playing the guessing game for patrons on where the exact slip or fall took place is simply creating a liability for your company where there was none.

Tapper's Tip #64

Taking photos of an area that your employee "thinks" made a patron fall, works against your interests. Unless that patron specifically points out the very spot where an incident happened, your employees should be prohibited from going on photographic safaris for their own versions of an incident.

And if a patron does take you to the exact spot of an incident, after the fact, be sure that your photograph is an accurate depiction of the condition of the scene *as of the time of the incident*. Additional hazards now showing (such as a vacuum cleaner cord stretched across the area from a maintenance person's clean-up operation) that weren't there when the slip/fall incident took place, should not appear in your photo. Attention to detail is extremely important.

Tapper's Tip #65

Incident reports are no place for subjective, opinionated comments of the person completing the report.

Example #2) EDITORIALIZING

You get no brownie points for writing things like this on an incident report: "I told the Facilities supervisor three times already to fix the leak in this restroom before somebody slips and hurts themselves." And beware of using vague reference words such as "small," "large," or "big," to refer to things like cuts or bruises, holes in a carpet, water on a floor, or puddles on a driveway. The word "big," or "small," is relative to something else, and what you might consider as big, another person could consider as small.

These kinds of words only confuse or make matters worse for the defense. At the time of trial two to six years later, your attorney will have to get the testimony of the person who wrote the report to define what "big" meant. Usually, that person doesn't remember anything other than what's on the report. If you're dealing with size references for a report, actually measure the item, or if you are taking a picture of the specific item (not the injured person), put a ruler with readable numbers in the photo for reference.

Also consider the problem you set for yourself in using the term "drunk" to describe a person's condition. Without specific details, it opens the door for harsh cross-examination of the incident report's writer at trial. "Drunk" is an opinion and conclusion that must be based on objective observations, such as "eyes were bloodshot," "unable to stand up on his own," "could not walk a straight line," "slurred his words," or "smelled of alcohol." Without the objective descriptions, the word "drunk" will backfire on your defense team.

Tapper's Tip #66

Incident reports are usually the only piece of evidence that a security or management person who filled out the report remembers about the event several years later. The report is their "recollection," so what's in it is an important element for preserving testimony and recollection for defense witnesses.

Every portion of an incident report can be a fertile breeding ground for words that backfire, not only on your company, but on the person in charge of filling out the reports. I've seen too many times how the authors of these reports get chewed up by vigorous cross-examination at trial because, other than what is specifically in the report, the authors tend to have no independent remembrance of the specific incident. Given that a trial can take place years after the incident, and hundreds of other incidents and investigations have taken place in that time period, it's no wonder there's little recollection. That's why it's so important to make the incident report work for you at the time it's prepared.

If your company's defense counsel has ever grimaced at what's in your incident reports, it's time to give serious attention to properly training your staff. Companies are, too often, intimidated into settling a case because of the damage potential from what their own employees put in, or leave out of, incident reports.

2-2. Surveillance Videos:
Candid camera works both ways.

Companies that have surveillance cameras feeding images to VCRs and digital recorders to cover activities of patrons have one of the best risk management devices you can buy to provide actual evidence of incidents and protection against fraudulent claims. In retail, hotel, and casino establishments, the "eye in the sky" is everywhere, and it significantly strengthens the defense of injury claims.

But there's a responsibility that accompanies the use of surveillance. If placed in areas where a person's expectation of privacy is invaded, such as restrooms, dressing rooms, or hotel rooms, you'll set yourself up for an invasion of privacy suit far worse than the injury claim you attempted to avoid. Even in common public areas, you should post a sign advising that surveillance is taking place to avoid claims of invasion of privacy. The mere announcement of active surveillance may also act as a deterrent to fraudulent injury claims and criminal activity.

Although surveillance is a major benefit in showing incidents, such as slips and falls as they happen, altercations, or thefts of purses and wallets, the tapes also record your security officers' speech and actions after they arrive on the scene. If your security people tend to "rough up" patrons where there has been no provocation for the use of force, other than some nasty words spoken by the patron, the tape will become your smoking gun. The same holds true when security people over-react in handcuffing a patron and the tape shows no need or reason for doing so. (Situations arise, of course, that don't fit neatly into "rules," because every incident is unique, and each security person's reaction is based on perception, discretionary judgment, experience, and training.)

In general, though, the ways to address this concern are threefold:

First, be sure the security officers you hire have a "clean" record from previous employment, free of assaults on people, or prior charges for excessive use of force, or disciplinary actions for insubordination, or other reasons that show overly aggressive behavior.

Second, define the mission of your security force in clear, understandable language. Are they there to deter crime, provide for guest safety, guest assistance, defend the company against criminals—all of the above, or some of the above? Establish priorities and make sure their behavior is in line with the priority.

Third, provide proper training in simulated conditions and demonstrate what are considered acceptable and unacceptable responses. The fact that many of the security personnel may come from police and law enforcement backgrounds makes them more attuned to responding to criminals than providing quality levels of customer service. Refresh and update the training frequently, based on actual incidents that occurred, not only in your company's establishments, but from the news of events in other places that can serve as examples.

If your company is conducting video or audio surveillance in areas where patrons are expecting privacy, such as in an "interrogation" room, where security personnel take people while awaiting arrival of local police authorities, or in a nurse's or first aid station where the patron is being treated, post the fact that such surveillance is taking place. Otherwise, you may open the door for a claim of invasion of privacy. It's a two-edged sword, though, to include surveillance in these areas, because if your security employees exceed their authority, or "forget" their training on how to conduct an investigative interview, your company will be producing and directing its own smoking gun. And you already know that all of your video and audio surveillance is discoverable.

SURVEILLING A PLAINTIFF IN HER OWN HOMETOWN:

On the other hand, when a plaintiff files a claim against your company, alleging her injury was caused by something your company or its employees did or failed to do, video surveillance of the plaintiff on her own turf by a private detective agency, can work wonders on producing a smoking gun that, for a change, backfires on the other side. Don't just do this without thought, though, as it could also backfire on you if you're in a jurisdiction where the existence of the tape must be disclosed, and produced, to the other side, regardless of what's on it and whether or not you intend to use it as evidence in the trial. Also, the professionalism and integrity of the people you engage to do this will be of utmost importance, particularly if you intend to rely on them for trial testimony.

When you engage these people, they will be considered your "agents," and you could be liable for their actions. That's why I suggest that you pursue this procedure only through your company's attorneys who know the local laws, and can assume the responsibility for engaging only qualified and reputable people in the field.

When done properly, the surveillance can sometimes strike gold. I remember a case where a plaintiff claimed that as a result of the defendant's negligence, she suffered "profound memory loss, debilitating headaches, chronic indigestion, and continual pain" that had her in a "catatonic" state. We hired a private investigator who shot two hours of surveillance tape showing the plaintiff playing golf and swinging the club quite freely, with no expression of pain, carrying heavy equipment to a camp site, getting in and out of a van, carrying shopping bags, and washing a car while laughing with friends.

Although this kind of surveillance was covert and allowable in the state where it took place, we had to disclose the videotape to the plaintiff's attorney because we intended to use it at trial. No matter. When you hit "gold" like this, it's an exhilarating day for the defense. It was satisfying to point the smoking gun in the plaintiff's direction for a change.

2-3. Evidence:Chain of Custody
Who will be the weakest link?

"Chain of custody" is a popular phrase in the world of evidence in criminal trials. It refers to accountability for the safekeeping of an item of evidence (a blood sample, or murder weapon, for example) by the person or "chain" of people who had possession or control ("custody") of it, from the time it was found or discovered, until it's produced and used at trial. If the chain is broken, and a "link" as to who had custody during any given time cannot be accounted for, an adversary can use that missing link to raise suspicion as to whether there was opportunity for someone to tamper with it. With enough suspicion, the jury perceives the item as an unreliable representation of its condition at the time it was first discovered.

The "chain of custody" issue is no different in civil litigation. It's an area that can backfire when you have an object, say a folding chair, that a person claims as the cause of her injury. Your inspection of the chair shows nothing wrong with it. That chair will be an important piece of evidence for your defense, and you'll want to produce it at trial to show the jury. If you don't have a way of safekeeping it, free of any tampering opportunities, a good trial lawyer may create an impression for the jury that someone repaired it since the time of the incident.

Tapper's Tip #67

If you're in a business that generates a large number of personal injury suits, don't ignore the "chain of custody" requirement to preserve your evidence. You need an inventory system with safekeeping procedures to retain and secure the evidence.

If the item is too large, or not practical to detach because it's part of a larger assembly, a photograph of the area or item in question will usually suffice. But to use the photograph as evidence, someone will usually have to testify that the scene or item depicted in the photo actually represents "the way it was" at the time of the mishap or incident. Be sure to secure that testimony.

The same principle applies to surveillance video tapes.

Tapper's Tip #68

If you intend to use in-house surveillance video as evidence in a trial, you'll be expected to retain the original "master" tape in safekeeping, under lock and key, with controls to assure an unbroken chain of custody from the time of the incident captured on video until trial.

In those industries that use video surveillance continuously, with multiple locations and recorders, the control of tape inventory is, indeed, a management challenge. Nonetheless, it's one that must be conquered. Typically, surveillance video tapes are recycled on a periodic basis, and re-used until an incident happens that may be the subject of litigation or a claim against the company. At that moment, in a well-managed system, the video operator will remove the tape from the recorder and place it in a "logged" inventory for safekeeping as potential evidence.

Tapper's Tip #69

When surveillance videos are used as evidence, the "master" (original) tape should never leave the possession of the person in custody of it, even when copies are made for lawyers.

The person in charge of the custody should have sole responsibility for copying the tape for those who may be entitled to see it. Not even the company's chief executive should be allowed to "borrow" the "master" for viewing purposes, unless the person responsible for its custody brings it to the showing, puts it into the VCR, remains in the room until it's finished, and takes it back with him for safekeeping. That way, the "master" tape never leaves the custody of its personal master.

2--4. Hiring an Expert: *Gem or surprise package?*

Ask trial lawyers about which element of litigation is the most costly (aside from their own fees) and you're likely to hear "the cost of experts." Your choice of an expert, however, can surprisingly backfire on you—particularly if you don't pin-down and become aware of either the expert's prior testimony in other cases, or her published books and articles that may contradict her present expert opinion on your behalf.

Tapper's Tip #70

Remember that trial lawyers have a "bank" of information on most of the top experts that companies use, over and over again, for testimony on specific issues. They can search their databases by using keywords, and pull up everything your expert has ever testified, or written, about. Be sure you do your own research so they don't bury your horse before he's out of the gate.

You might call in an expert and celebrate when her opinion puts your company in a very favorable light on crucial issues at trial. But if you don't know that she testified in a similar situation five years ago and took a different position for another client, your surprise will come during cross-examination. While she's testifying on your behalf in front of a jury, the plaintiff's trial lawyer—armed with his keyword search in the "document bank" that finds all of her prior testimony in other cases—will chew her up and spit her out during cross.

When you hire an expert your company hasn't used before, a background search should include former testimony given by that expert in any previous trial. You need to know the issues that were involved in those prior trials, whether the expert testified for the plaintiff or the defense, and any articles, books, or other publications the expert has authored or co-authored. Don't overlook testimony the expert may have given in deposition transcripts, even if the case involved never went to trial, as you can never be sure that an attorney, as a member of one of the attorney information networks, hasn't posted those transcripts for sharing on one of those network Web sites.

Become a partner with your outside counsel on selecting an expert for use at trial and share the obligation of doing a "due diligence" review of the expert's prior activities.

Tapper's Tip #71

Don't rely only on the expert's summary about prior case involvement, the nature of prior testimony given, articles written, or statements made in public interviews. Get the names of cases and sources of all previously published statements. Ask the expert for copies of all prior transcripts of testimony, and all other published materials, and if not available, check out independent sources to acquire them. Read them all, and be sure there's nothing contradictory to the present opinion of the expert.

I recall what happened at one of the nationally televised trials in Florida during the 2000 presidential election battle between Bush and Gore. The Bush team was trying to establish that the dimples on a punch card that registered no vote for a presidential candidate were the result of voter choice, not an inadequately maintained machine that housed the punch-card ballot.

Testimony revealed that the little pieces of paper that resulted from pushing a hole through the punch-card ballot (the "chads") accumulated inside the "machines" which, in some cases, were not cleaned out for years. The theory of the Gore team was that these "chads" filled the machines' reservoirs and backed up behind the location where the holes would be punched for choosing a presidential candidate, resulting in a voter erroneously thinking that he punched a hole, although it didn't penetrate completely through.

The Bush team produced the actual inventor of the particular punch card ballot machine as an expert witness. After testifying very favorably that the accumulation of chads in the reservoir would not affect the ability to penetrate a punch hole in a ballot, the inventor was hit (and so was the Bush team) with a surprise attack in cross-examination. The Gore side had an investigative team at the U.S. Patent and Trademark Office in Washington, D.C., scrutinizing the records on file for this inventor's patent. To their own surprise, they found that he had filed an application for a new patent for an "improved" version of the punch card ballot machine that he had invented.

As part of the application, he had signed an affidavit that detailed the reasons why this was an improvement over the previous patent. In it, he mentioned how "chads" in the existing machine had a tendency to accumulate and, potentially, clog the machine, which could result in punch card impressions that didn't go all the way through. This had the "potential" of causing the machines that read and tallied the ballots to register them as "no votes."

Here was an affidavit—a public record, and statement under oath—that contradicted the inventor's own present testimony. He tried to wiggle out of the contradiction when the Bush attorneys attempted to repair the damage. The well-seasoned and competent lawyers on the Bush team appeared surprised, although they acted deftly to hide it. Did they know about this in advance? I doubt it. If they had known, they would have brought it up during the direct questioning of their expert to deny the Gore team its surprise attack.

2-5. The Company "On Notice":
Knock, knock...is anybody there?

REGULATORY NOTICES

It would almost seem obvious that when your company

receives a notice of non-compliance or violation from any governmental or other regulatory agency, a response and follow-up is imperative. But believe it or not, as obvious as it is, too many companies have no formalized system for organizing and centralizing this information. When your company is sued, a plaintiff's lawyer will serve subpoenas on all relevant regulatory agencies for copies of correspondence or notices advising of violations, or fines, involving your company, and questions will arise if notices turn up from the agencies, but not from your own files.

The failure to find these notices in the company's files will usually stem from a poor filing system or lack of a centralized procedure. When you can't find the notices, you may discover that, indeed, notices were received, but the current supervisor of the responsible department advises that "someone else" was supposed to take care of them, but that "someone" is no longer in the company's employ. Alternatively, the current supervisor will tell you that those violations occurred under the watch of her predecessor, who never informed her of these problems; the predecessor, of course, is no longer with the company. It reminds me of the shell game where you hide the pea under one of three shells and you keep moving the shells around trying to guess where it is. Everybody, it seems, has a reason or excuse why the notices aren't available, or why the violations weren't corrected.

When the plaintiff's lawyer shows the jury official notices of violations to which your company did not respond, or for which you have no record of responding, that can portray an air of arrogance to a jury. And "arrogance" is a key ingredient that moves jurors toward the desire to award punitive damages to the plaintiff.

Tapper's Tip #72

Always follow-up, in writing, to any notices from regulatory authorities, and never close the file until all issues have been handled.

Tapper's Tip #73

Set up procedures to funnel all official notices from any regulatory authority directly to your law department or to one central department and designated person. That person should be assigned the responsibility and accountability for coordinating the entire response, including corrective action, if any. Responsibility without accountability means nothing.

CUSTOMER COMPLAINTS AS "NOTICE"

Whether your company does or doesn't have a consumer relations office, the problem in this area concerns lack of controls for follow-up on issues brought to your attention by your customers. People whose departments are affected by criticism tend to protect their job functions and react to outside complaints with suspicion, as if they were an unjustified attack on the quality of their work or service. You need to look for the bigger picture when consumers alert you to potential defects in your products.

Tapper's Tip #74

All of your customers' complaints by telephone, e-mails, or letters are discoverable, and if your company cannot show that it gave appropriate time and effort to address the issues, those complaints will become smoking guns that prove your company was "on notice."

You should, therefore, adopt procedures for complaints to be handled centrally, funneled to the appropriate department head for response. If complaints allege a link between your product and serious injuries or deaths, you'd better conduct an objective review (by those who aren't part of the "inside" group in management, because the "insiders" are usually too closely attached to the issues) to determine if the "link" has merit. And you need to do this without regard to the costs or consequences of the findings.

If you don't tackle the problem in a timely way, you'll fall into the pit that trapped the Firestone Tire and Ford Motor companies. Firestone was forced to recall 6.5 million tires in 2000 for tread separations, and Ford spent billions to recover from a public relations debacle involving its close association with Firestone, after over 200 deaths were attributed to Firestone tire failures and rollover accidents on Ford Explorers and Mountaineers. I'll give you the details of those situations in Chapter 9.

LITIGATION AS "NOTICE"

Just as customer complaints put the company "on notice" of problems, lawsuits lodged against your company have the same effect.

Lawsuits are public records and plaintiffs in most jurisdictions are entitled to question, through pre-trial discovery methods, the circumstances of those prior suits. If your company was successful in "winning" them, the judgments or verdicts in your favor provide a record of no wrongdoing. But if your company settled those prior suits by paying money to the opponents, or if it suffered an adverse verdict, those cases are "notices" of problems. Did you take action to fix the problems or issues raised? Did you establish any new procedures, or revise old ones, to prevent the same type of incidents from happening again? Did you re-train any of your employees or conduct new training exercises since then?

Punitive damages are based on a finding of a company's "reckless" and "wanton" disregard for the safety of those people affected by a product or service. If you take no reasonable action to prevent prior history from repeating itself, you're playing right into the trial lawyer's battle plan.

Tapper's Tip #75

If your company was a defendant in prior lawsuits, use the claims made in those suits as learning tools to correct whatever gave rise to them. Don't let history repeat itself.

2-6. Laptops and Desktops Discarded:
Junkyard dogs or bounty of gold?

As companies upgrade their technology and increase their sophistication of multimedia presentations, there's a need to replace the old desktops and the slower laptops with newer, faster

ones that can handle the demands for processing these fea-
tures. But where do these "old" computers go? Is there a
junkyard heaven? Do you have a room in your Information
Technology area that serves the purpose? Perhaps, it's larger
than that, a warehouse. Maybe your company holds on to some
of its outdated computers to cannibalize them for parts, while
donating others that are fully functional to charitable organizations or needy schools.

Typically, people from the Information Technology area
remove the old computers and install the new ones, but what
formal system does your company have in place to assure that
the hard drives are removed and sanitized from these discards?

Tapper's Tip #76

Adopt strict control procedures, as a matter of security, to assure
the prompt removal and cleaning of all hard drives from laptops
and desktops that have been removed from "active" duty. Make
someone accountable for consistent enforcement. Don't risk getting caught with a bunch of "old" hard drives with discernible information you would have to produce in future pre-trial discovery.

Plaintiffs' forensic experts would have a field day with
them. Who knows what golden nuggets they'd find, but you
can almost bet they will, indeed, find some. And if any of these
old computers wind up in the trash heap, imagine the trea-
sures your competitors can discover using the same techniques,
all perfectly legal, when your trash becomes public property.

Let's be clear on what's meant by "cleaning" the hard drives.
I'm not talking about just deleting existing files. You need to use
a software program that "cleans" the drives and wipes them clear
of not just all current files, but all of the "deleted" ones and

their remnants that have not yet been overwritten. This also means the removal of all software programs, including the operating system itself, so the drive, when finished, will be as "empty" as a new one fresh out of the box.

If a drive is broken and removed from your PC because it's no longer functional, don't ignore the fact that lots of your important data are still residing on the disk inside the drive. You'll need to take appropriate steps to capture what you must keep, and destroy the remaining data. I'll leave it to your Information Technology people to best figure out how to accomplish that.

Be sure to realize, however, that nothing should get deleted unless it's part of your established procedures in a document retention policy. The remnants and old files on these discarded drives should be included in that policy.

Chapter 4

PART THREE

EMPLOYMENT

3-1. Web Bulletin Boards: *Who's watching?*

Does your company support a bulletin or message board that employees can access directly from their office computers and remotely from home computers? This is where employees can communicate with each other, post personal ads, seek information, and generally converse.

Tapper's Tip #77

If your company sponsors or lends support to a Web bulletin board, it would be wise to monitor it to protect against misuse of confidential information and posting of inappropriate comments about co-employees. Establish clear and specific rules and manners for posting, and enforce them with discipline for violators.

To the extent the company has some connection in supporting the electronic board as a communication tool, the comments posted can subject the company to claims of hostile environment, sexual harassment, discrimination, and even defamation.

In a ground-breaking case in New Jersey (*Blakey vs. Continental Airlines, Inc.*, June 1, 2000), that state's Supreme Court declared that a company in New Jersey may be liable for fostering a hostile environment, or condoning sexual harassment by what takes place on a Web-based bulletin board exclusive to the company's employees. Although the company had no "duty" to monitor the exchanges between employees, it could still be liable if its management had knowledge that offensive behavior was taking place on the board, and it failed to take effective remedial measures to end it. The fact that the "board" was outside the physical workplace didn't matter, so long as what took place there affected the environment inside.

In this case, the plaintiff was a female pilot who complained that defamatory remarks about her were posted by other pilots on the company's Web bulletin board. This is the same site where the company maintained its flight crew information, such as pilot pairings and its crew member schedules, and expected its pilots and crew to take their assignments from it.

The high court said a jury would have to decide if Continental, as a company, should be considered as having had knowledge of the defamatory messages because its Chief Pilots, who used the Web forum, were "managerial" level employees and representatives of the company.

Interestingly, the Court didn't perceive any critical difference between a bulletin board of the wood and cork variety, hanging in a work lounge, and one that's electronically posted on the Internet. The point is clear: a Web-based site for employees only, can be considered just as much a part of the workplace, regardless of its physical location. In my view, if your company sets up an exclusively dedicated Internet message forum, it better be prepared to monitor all activity there, legal duty or not.

3-2. Physical Surroundings: *Look and ye shall offend*

Look around your office, hallways, break rooms, and other offices. Do you see any postings on bulletin boards, pictures on walls, magnetic caricatures on file cabinets, signs, printouts, cartoons or sticky notes taped to office doors, or on the fronts or sides of computer monitors that might have any connotation of sex, discriminatory images or language based on age, national origin, religion, or physical appearance?

Employment lawsuits are now as commonplace as slip-and-fall and workers' comp cases. Employees are not shy about suing a company for maintaining a "hostile work environment," even while they're still employed. A supervisor's or co-worker's off-color comments may warrant a "sexual harassment" claim. Even your failure to promote an employee brings cries of discrimination of some proscribed type (sexual, racial, religious, or based on national origin). It's tough enough to defend these suits when traditional community views tend to favor the individual against big business. Why support such employees' claims with physical evidence sitting on your desk or attached to your walls that can be misinterpreted and twisted to their advantage?

Tapper's Tip #78

Check your office's surroundings and sanitize them from all pictures, posters, cartoons, or quotations that can be twisted, tweaked, or tortured into misinterpretation. They can play into a disgruntled employee's hands for an employee lawsuit based on sexual harassment, hostile environment, or discrimination. Do it now to avoid a potentially high-costing smoking gun.

Take, for instance, an office I visited several years ago where the light switch on the wall was covered by a switch plate in the form of a cartoon caricature of a smiling boy with baggy pants. The fly on his pants was open and cut out for the toggle switch to fit through, so each time you turned the lights on and off, you, of course, had to flick the switch. The supervisor, whose office I was in, had a great laugh when I noticed it. Maybe, in a different place and time, it might be amusing, but in the workplace, especially in today's environment, where actions and words are fragile for misinterpretation, there's no place for it. Here, whatever training the company gave to its supervisors simply didn't sink in.

Just imagine someone in that department bringing a lawsuit against the supervisor and the company for sexual harassment incidents, unrelated to the switch. How do you think the switch plate will play in court as supportive evidence of the environment? If the plaintiff's lawyer discovers it, photographs it, or better yet, videotapes a female turning the switch on and off in close-up view, and displays it to the jury on a 50 inch projection screen, how will the company's vice-president look while on the stand testifying about the "no tolerance" policy for sexual harassment?

What about cartoons posted on walls and bulletin boards? Do they poke fun at blondes? At racial differences? At religious practices? They're no different than the switch plate, so take them down! Sanitize your workplace with totally generic postings, if you must have them at all. Post pictures of your company's logo or products, or news articles about your company, motivational team posters, or pictures of employees at the company picnic (provided they're not suggestive in any way of the prohibited areas already covered.)

Some years ago, in a case in Illinois, a hotel resort was sued because its security staff allegedly roughed up, and ousted, a patron who was inebriated and disturbing other guests in the lobby. The issue was whether the security guard used excessive force. The hotel denied the allegations and contended their security personnel acted reasonably at all times. During a recess of several days in the trial, the plaintiff's lawyer personally delivered, and served on the security department's Chief of Security, a subpoena for records he needed.

Normally, this is a routine event, but the lawyer was escorted to the Chief's security office where he could serve the subpoena. He was invited in, and guess what was on the wall behind the Chief's desk? A full-size baseball bat, glued onto a large wooden plaque, with "The Convincer" prominently painted across the bat. The lawyer called the in-house counsel for the hotel and demanded the right to photograph the plaque, or bring it to court for when the trial resumed. The in-house counsel had never been inside the Chief's office before, so he was caught unaware. The case never resumed trial. It settled for an undisclosed sum.

Think defensively, and stay away from all accessories that might support a prospective lawsuit, even if to do so would require an interpretation that's distorted or manipulated in some way. Don't underestimate a potential opponent. Consider the other side's strategy by visualizing each advantage it can muster out of your physical surroundings. Then, remove all such advantages. That will level the playing field, and you, too, will not only be smart, but working smarter.

3-3. Performance Evaluations:
Straighten up and fly right.

With the exploding numbers of employees filing lawsuits based on allegations of age, race, or sexual discrimination, or retaliatory demotions or firings, the written annual performance evaluation may become the central piece of evidence that could aid or destroy a company's defense. It depends on how supervisors and other managers are trained in the art of completing the evaluation.

Tapper's Tip #79

Use of inappropriate slang, or demeaning words, to describe what's wrong with an employee's performance, can mean the difference between winning or losing an employment lawsuit as a defendant. Experts, who are knowledgeable on all the nuances of employment law, should provide training sessions to every manager who is required to fill out employee evaluation forms.

Too many managers consider the evaluation summary as a "chore," so they fill it out perfunctorily, not taking the time to speak to an employee's peers to get feedback on performance issues. Putting a lot of fluff, puff, and accolades in the evaluation to stay on a "friendly," working basis, actually does a disservice to the employee who never really knows the true perception of his work, much less what he can do to improve upon it.

And it does a major disservice to the company when layoff time comes, and you have to dismiss the employee. If there's "cause" for a layoff, and you had given a gushing, inflated evaluation of the employee just a few months earlier, you bought yourself a lot of explaining to do for the company when it's defending the employment suit. Be ready for the employee's trial lawyer to wave that evaluation in your face.

> ### Tapper's Tip #80
>
> Be realistic in your write-ups on an employee's performance. Deal directly with the issues of strengths and weaknesses, so the employee can seize opportunities to improve. Don't exaggerate your statements or give praise where it's not earned.

If the employee is part of a team and there are things common to the team that need improvement, be consistent in your evaluations of all its members to avoid a claim that you're discriminating against any one of them. Always try to back up your statements of "need for change" with examples from the employee's performance.

3-4. Background Checks: *Flushing out the weeds.*

The standard background check verifies employment history, education, and references. But you should take it a step further. Be sure to get authorization, in advance, from the employee-candidate, at the time he fills out the application for employment, to request a criminal background check and any other "record" check, such as a driving record, if it relates to the job functions and responsibilities.

For example, if you have valet parkers, shuttle drivers, or delivery truck drivers, you'll want a driver's history record to verify any moving violations and "points," including charges of driving under the influence. For security personnel, you'll want, at the very least, a criminal history record, and an employment verification as to whether the person was ever involved in disciplinary proceedings at a prior job for using excessive force, insubordination, or assaults and batteries. If you hire consultants who are about to be shown trade secrets and other highly confidential information, wouldn't you want to do a background check to verify the consultant was not involved in a former or present lawsuit against him for misappropriation of trade secrets, or violations of non-compete contracts of his former employers?

Suppose your company employs valet parkers. While driving a customer's car to the parking area, the valet parker hits a lady walking across the circular drive to your premises. If the attorney for the lady discovers that your company never did a background check, before or after hiring this valet driver, and the driver had two convictions for driving under the influence, and one for reckless driving involving a pedestrian, you'd better get your checkbook out; time to throw in the towel to avoid the negative public relations, let alone the inevitable liability.

Tapper's Tip #81

Good risk management practice requires that your company set required standards of compliance with driving laws for all employees who drive vehicles in a "safety-related" function, such as valet parking, shuttling people to and from an airport or hotel, or surveilling a parking area. This would require the employee's dismissal if a driving record exceeded a maximum number of "points," or maximum number of moving citations, or violations, such as "driving under the influence."

But merely setting up standards is not enough. They're only effective if you have a system in place to update the driving records at designated intervals. If you don't assign follow-up responsibility to ensure an employee's continued compliance with your standards, that failure is as much a smoking gun as having no policy at all. Here, "actions" count more than words.

Other employees for whom background checks (not limited to driving records) are advisable would include those in maintenance, housekeeping (for hotels), commercial deliveries, first-aid assistance, recreational activities (such as in arcades, swimming pools, or outdoor amusements), front desk positions in hotels (where access to room keys provides opportunities), quality control supervisory roles, food preparation, drug manufacturing, and, of course, any activity involving care, custody, or supervision of minor children.

In Memphis, Tennessee, on April 5, 2002, the local T.V. news and print headlines screamed of a day care van that ran off the highway and hit an embankment, killing the driver and four young children. Investigators found the driver had prior convictions for drug use which should have kept him from a job behind the wheel, based on state regulations. Prior to this tragedy, the children had reported him for smoking marijuana while driving them to and from. The daycare center had never done a background check on its driver. With no surprise, lawsuits against the owners of the center were filed promptly after the tragedy.

Tapper's Tip #82

Don't overlook the benefit of a background check on every employee your company hires. And if you're in an industry that requires such checks as mandatory, make sure you perform them with due diligence, and follow all state regulatory requirements. Without those precautions, your defense against a claim of negligent hiring will be feeble, at best, heading you in the direction of a hefty punitive damage verdict.

A company's failure to check out the background of new hires is a smoking gun for headline news if any of those employees cause injury or death to customers or co-workers, particularly if their background includes an arrest record for drug-related or violent crimes.

Chapter 4

PART FOUR
INFRASTRUCTURE

4-1. Parent/Subsidiary Relations:
Love me or leave me?

For a variety of reasons, large companies do business through a number of different corporations (each a subsidiary, or "sub") whose ownership is tied to one main company (the parent). Usually the parent company owns all or a majority of the shares of stock in the subsidiary.

Two significant reasons for doing business through a subsidiary are to take advantage of tax savings on federal and state levels, and to insulate the parent company from liability for the subsidiary's debts and operations. In theory, the stockholders are not liable for the corporation's obligations, so when the parent company is the sole stockholder and thus, owner, of the subsidiary corporation, the parent company gets the benefits of ownership without the liability. But the theory assumes that each corporation is an independent entity, separate and apart from its stockholders, not just an extension of them.

What the law requires to insulate a parent corporation from liability for its wholly-owned subsidiary is to show that the subsidiary truly does operate separate and apart from its parent. If the sub has too many ties to the parent, in terms of the parent's "control," the law will ignore the separate corporate identities and hold the parent-owner accountable for the obligations and wrongdoings of the sub.

Suppose, for example, a plaintiff is injured by a product manufactured by a subsidiary. The plaintiff sues both the subsidiary and the parent company that owns the sub to attempt to hold them jointly liable as defendants. (A plaintiff's attorney prefers to get a verdict against the parent company because it usually has a "deeper pocket" to pay a large verdict.) The parent company tries to get out of the suit as promptly as it can. To do this, it has to assert that it neither directed, nor controlled, the actions or operations of the sub. But the words and actions of the managers of the "parent," and the managers of the sub, may have undermined the "theory" of independence. Through sloppy structuring of the companies, inattentiveness to details of "independence," or lax management, the arrangement for "separate and apart" liability backfires!

Here are the blunders:

COMMON BOARDS AND OFFICERS- Instead of making sure the sub has independent directors and officers, those who set up the internal structure of the companies appoint the same boards of directors and officers for both parent and sub.

COMMON BANKING OPERATIONS-Sometimes the parent-owner and the sub share the same banking operations and bank accounts, with separation occurring only on paper for accounting purposes. Funding for the sub comes from the parent, to the extent the sub doesn't have sufficient operating income.

USING PARENT'S NAME INDISCRIMINATELY-By entering into contracts with vendors for supplies, and consultants for professional services, managers set the stage for a backfire when they use the parent's corporate name as the contracting party on contracts where the services or supplies are solely for the sub. The parent becomes contractually bound for the sub's obligations.

Tapper's Tip #83

Interlacing relationships between parent and subsidiary don't, in and of themselves, destroy the separate treatment and identity of the corporations. It's the number of such relationships that takes you over the threshold of "separateness" and into the realm of "direction and control." When it's "one for all, and all for one" in the real operation, you're on thin ice trying to insulate the parent from liability.

USE OF PARENT'S STATIONERY-Not wanting to spend the money for separate letterhead, the sub uses the parent company's letterhead.

SHARING EQUIPMENT OF PARENT WITHOUT FORMALITIES-Sharing equipment, such as delivery vehicles and service vans belonging to the parent, without setting up the "separate and apart" formalities of a lease or sharing arrangement, as you would if you had borrowed or leased them from a third party, undermines independence.

Tapper's Tip #84

Pay attention to the formalities of operating parent and subsidiary as two independent companies. The more indicia of "control" a trial lawyer can find on the parent, in its relation to the subsidiary, the greater chance those controls will become the smoking guns to destroy the credibility of the parent's vigorous assertions of independence.

To strengthen the parent's defense of no liability, be sure the employees who negotiate contracts, execute purchase orders and prepare memos, correspondence and reports, know exactly which business entity to use for formal transactions. You need keen oversight and coordination between management and the legal department, combined with effective training and workshops for all management personnel.

Tapper's Tip #85

When you blur the distinctions, in use of letterhead, in sloppy references in contracts, particularly in the name of the contracting party, and in memos that show clearly how the parent company's officers and key management are "directing," or setting, policy for the subsidiary, the courts will find the sub as the "alter-ego" of the parent, and hold the parent liable for the sub's obligations.

The alter-ego principle is actually derived from a doctrine called "piercing the corporate veil," where the veil refers to the protective cloak around the owners (shareholders) of a corporation that shields them from liability for its debts and activities. A court can pierce the corporate veil in cases where shareholders form a corporation and use it to commit fraudulent or illegal acts. The alter-ego principle recognizes the corporate "front" as a sham, and holds the shareholders liable, regardless of whether those shareholders are corporations or individuals.

S.E.C. REPORTING- A POTENTIAL TRAP?

The loose distinction between parent and sub poses another potentially devastating backfire. If the parent is a public company, registered on a stock exchange, and the officers, auditors, or the parent company's attorneys, are aware of the common management and "alter-ego" relationship with its sub, the parent company might be obliged to disclose the potential liabilities of the sub, as those of the parent, on the annual required filings with the Securities and Exchange Commission. This is just to avoid a misrepresentation in the parent's financial reports. Your attorneys would have to decide if the arrangements are so close to a finding of "alter-ego" status that certain of your financial reports might be misleading under federal securities laws if they didn't report, at least as a footnote, the significant liabilities of the sub as a potential, or contingent, obligation of the publicly-held parent.

Chapter 5

The Paper Shuffle

Managing the "paper trail"

Do you ever feel overwhelmed by paper coming at you in all directions? Your In-Box piles up faster than a snow drift in a blizzard, and you can't shovel it away fast enough to fill your Out-Box. No sooner do you tackle the pile-up, there's more on its way.

You just get started on tackling this avalanche when your colleagues or staff members drop by, either to say hello in passing, or to mention some "hot news" of internal politics in the company. And then, it's time to attend the corporate meeting that you first got wind of a couple of hours ago. Maybe it's time for your own weekly staff meeting, a departmental meeting, or a continuing progress meeting for a special project assignment. While you're away, you know what's happening back at your desk,

don't you? That paper snow pile keeps getting bigger and bigger. When you return, you think you might be "snowed-in" for
the night.

Welcome to "The Paper Shuffle" of the corporate world!

Among the paper that's accumulating are all sorts of
information, some of it junk, some of it the "Who has time for
this?" variety. Those can be set aside. But the loads of
correspondence, memos, reports, or analyses containing
substantive company information, a fair amount of which is
"confidential," can't be ignored. Much of it is certainly not
intended for public distribution, and more likely, intended for a
limited audience.

With the hassle of everyday activity, how organized are you
in processing this information overload, and particularly, the
confidential material? If you're like most of us, the "organization"
is more like "disorganization." Indeed, the key is discipline with
attention to details. But who has the time when it keeps coming
at you so fast? The key: You've got to MAKE the time!

Look around you, because we're about to take a tour of your
office area. We're looking for traps that breach confidentiality.
You may be surprised, and alarmed, to learn that you're already
in one or more of them. The bad news is: You don't know how
much you've already compromised by a sloppy or disorganized
workplace.

The good news is: YOU CAN CLEAN UP YOUR ACT, and
stop compromising confidentiality from this day forward. And
you can do it without much detection—unless your office is so
unkempt that your cleanup, and tidiness, will arouse suspicion
as to what came over you. People may think you're getting ready
to quit. If so, that only shows how far away you were from
managing confidential information "the right way." With some
good organizational work habits, you can be on your way as a
role model on how to manage your work product and handle the
corporate paper shuffle, without becoming the cause of future

problems. I'm not here to tell you how to organize; there's a hundred or more books on that topic. I'm here to save you from yourself—from mishandling confidential information. So, LISTEN UP!

Your Desktop

If you're like a majority of people, you won't want to save, or display, a picture of your desktop at the end of the day. Are file folders piled up, and loose papers, memos, and "stuff" you're working on all over the place? Are you at a loss to find an empty space to put a file or a paper that you know you'll need real soon? Even though it appears disorganized or disheveled, in your view there's "order" to this mess. "They just don't understand my system," you say, as you reach for the pile on the right, fumble through the stack, and grab just the paper you're looking for.

Of all the files and loose papers easily visible and accessible on top, on the floor, on tables, and anywhere else your office has a place to stack them, how much confidential information is in them? Be honest with yourself. Determine which of these papers or files would put you in a serious predicament if someone walked into your office when you weren't there and read, copied, or even took some. Imagine what would happen if copies of these papers found their way to your company's competitors, or to people in your own company not authorized to see them.

Tapper's Tip #86

Don't keep papers and files open and accessible to those who may enter your office in your absence. You'll destroy confidentiality, and breach confidentiality agreements with third parties.

Nothing—and I mean nothing!—should be left out and

exposed if it's confidential. This includes the material you have yet to see in your IN-Box, and that which has not yet been taken by your secretary from the OUT-Box for filing or distribution. At the end of the day, your desk area and office area should be devoid of files and extraneous papers. And that doesn't mean putting them into one big collection drawer without a lock. If the information is confidential (and let's face it, most of it is, if you think in terms of what you would not want "others" to see), you need to file it in "To Do" or "To Read" files that are kept in locked cabinets or drawers.

Secretaries' desks

The same observation (and warning) about visible and accessible papers on your own desk and surrounding areas applies to the desk and office areas of secretaries. Your paper management policy should, and must, apply to all secretaries, too. So don't just clean out your desk area by putting a bunch of "stuff" onto a secretary's desk. You will have only moved the location of the mess without tending to the security issue. Be scrupulous about enforcing the rules for everybody.

Tapper's Tip #87

What's on a secretary's desk is just as important as what's on an executive's. Oversee the confidentiality requirements with the same diligence.

Shared printer stations

The idea of a shared printer station, where the computers in an office area are wired into one printer, provides a potential trap that will breach confidentiality.

Tapper's Tip #88

Shared printer stations bust confidentiality. Get your own printer if you're involved in producing or downloading a lot of confidential material.

Here's what can typically happen in this situation. You're sent a confidential e-mail attachment that's a memo directing you to downsize your department by a certain date. You need to print it out, so you hit "print" on your e-mail program and it's on its way to the shared printer. But before you can get to the printer, the phone rings, and your caller I.D. screen shows it's your boss, so you leap to take the call. Before you're done with the call, three other people in the work area who share the same printer all hit "print" on their word processors and jump to the printer to get their documents. Anticipating their pages are coming through, they pick up the pages that are printing out, and each time they do, they get to see what's not their business, and more particularly, they get to see your "confidential" e-mail that's printing while you're busy talking to your boss.

The problem poses even more risks in a law department of a large company. If you have an in-house law department, and the members share a printer station with non-lawyers, documents intended to be attorney-client privileged material, but viewable by others, may lose their privileged status through such an arrangement. Law department managers need to be scrupulous in providing personal printers for those people working on privileged or other confidential material.

Make sure you evaluate the shared printer arrangements in your offices to determine who in your department may warrant his own "private" printer for confidentiality purposes. If you produce a lot of confidential documents in the course of your day, you should insist on having your very own printer in your office space, to provide a higher level of protection.

Tapper's Tip #89

Beware of outsiders who have access to your office area, including the janitorial service crew, and any other service people who enter your office premises.

Janitorial crews

Has anyone given any thought to the background of the janitorial service people who have carte blanche access to your offices in the evening, when no one is around? In fact, many of these cleaning services have such turnover in crews, it may be hard to catch up with the specific persons who cleaned your offices on any given night.

Did you know that in the business of corporate espionage (some refer to it, euphemistically, as "competitive intelligence"), private detective services, hired by competitors, have solicited the services of cleaning crew members to obtain information and materials from targeted companies while they clean? It's considerably easy to do: the janitorial service person looks for, and picks up, a specific paper or file folder which has been identified in advance, and copies the contents for the private firm. Or, the original papers could be removed, delivered to a private agency for review, and brought back the next evening, after they've been copied. In an office with large stacks of files all over, one file may not be noticed, particularly if it turns up the next day, and wasn't called for before then. It's no secret that these private agencies "plant" new hires in janitorial service companies for the purpose of getting access to the offices of the company they're interested in.

Failure to verify backgrounds of janitorial service people is a serious hole in your security blanket. These people have access to so much personal and confidential information, it's incredible! Your diaries and calendars, if left on your desks or in your unlocked desk drawers, are easy enticements. And I'm not only talking about the office cubicles in the general floor area. I'm talking about offices of the CEO, and other key managers, even the offices of the attorneys in the legal department.

Tapper's Tip #90

To the extent permissible, check out backgrounds of all service people as you would your own "new hires." Insist that service companies provide that information to you as part of vendor negotiations.

Not long ago, I had an appointment at a high-rise office center complex, where the ground floor offices at the front of the building all had floor-to-ceiling, plate glass windows. A walkway took me past each of these office windows. I arrived early in the morning, an hour before any offices opened, and as I walked around the outside of the building, I could see inside all of the front offices. They had no blinds or drapes over the vast, windowed areas.

I was astonished at what I saw as I passed by a security brokerage firm, with clear view inside. File folders of clients were stacked haphazardly, at least a foot high, in five different piles, on the floor surrounding a broker's desk. More files were on top of the desk, and even more were on a conference table in front of it. You couldn't see the wood finish of the desktop because that, too, was covered in loose papers and more files. Sticky reminder notes sloppily framed the computer monitor. I was surprised not to see an empty pizza box nearby.

I thought of all the clients who took comfort in believing that the personal information they gave to their broker was sound and secure, protected for privacy. Yet, there it was, "ripe for the pickin's," by any janitorial or utility service with access to the office, and, of course, any private firm that may have planted people in these service companies to acquire competitive information.

I know this brokerage operation is subject to federal laws designed to protect the privacy of personal consumer information, and those laws require it to send formal notices to consumer-clients to inform them of the steps it takes to protect it. The formal Privacy Notice usually says something like this:

> *"We maintain procedural safeguards, through physical protection and computer technology, that comply with federal standards to guard your nonpublic personal information."*

Imagine a lawyer representing a client whose personal information was pilfered from that brokerage firm. Now, assume the lawyer took a picture of the same scene I saw through the window. That photo would be the only smoking gun he would need. In contrast with the language of the Privacy Notice sent to the clients, he could nail that company into settling before trial. What an easy mark!

These are foolish, and negligent, business practices. And, so unnecessary—the result of business people unaware, or simply lackadaisacal, about the breeding ground right in front of their eyes. Yet, when trouble comes knocking, the managers will still react with surprise. I've seen the reaction too many times.

My concern about service people penetrating your

information network is not limited to the janitorial service industry. I'm not suggesting that people on janitorial crews are more unscrupulous or untrustworthy than other service groups. The same gaps in security present themselves with any service people who enter an office environment. Unfettered access could be the weakest link in your company's security chain for risk management purposes. It's not a "person" focus. It's a focus on access, opportunity, and availability.

Many companies have excellent reputations, and they're hired for that reason. They're also bonded with insurance protection to pay for loss or damage to "property" caused by their workers. But have you ever read the fine print? The "property" is usually defined in the "furniture, fixtures, and equipment" category. What about losses from misappropriation of data? You may want to check the coverage language of their policies more closely if you think there's comfort there. Maybe your own company has business insurance to cover trade secret theft.

But even if your company, or the service company, has it, the potential damage goes beyond reimbursement payments from an insurance company. How can you measure the loss in dollars when the news media does a "scoop" on your company, and you don't know how your company's sensitive information got into its hands? By the time you decipher how they got hold of it, the damage to your name and brand may have already occurred, not to mention the violation felt by your consumers whose personal information was compromised.

If you're still thinking "insurance," think about future arguments over definitions of coverage. Do you really want to be entwined for several years in a lawsuit with the insurance company, wrangling over whether you were covered for the loss, and whether you can prove monetary damages related to the misappropriation of confidential information? Remember, lawsuit filings are public records. The media will pick up the details for an embarrassing story about your mishandling of consumers' personal information, inadequate procedures to assure its security from outsiders, and the absence of real internal controls to protect it, contrasted against your assurances to customers each day on how you carefully guard their personal information. When those headlines hit, the class-action hounds will be beating a path to your door as if it were red meat in a famine! And your business will nose dive into a tailspin.

I've been in business, and counselor to businesses, for a long time, and realize that we have to take risks and live with assumptions. One such assumption is that if you pick a reputable service company, it does its own able job of screening its personnel. Well, that's supposed to be so, but how secure is your company in relying on that assumption, particularly in today's post-9/11 world? And what about the situation where you have no say in choosing the service people because they come with the "common area" fees that are part of your office rent? The owner or property manager for the office complex chooses them. How much reliance do you want to place on the owner or manager, and what do you know about their preferences and policies?

It's a question of how much risk you're willing to assume for the potential of compromising your customers' private information. How important is the protection of your customer database, your marketing plans, or the new product development files? What would it cost, in terms of crisis management, if this information were compromised? Is it worth your effort to take control of checking into the background of these outsiders who have carte blanche access to your offices? Because of laws protecting the privacy of employee information, you may have to make the revelation of employees' backgrounds a negotiating point in hiring the vendor. That vendor would have to get consent from its employees to allow you to see those files. By raising the issue, at least, you'll make the vendor more vigilant, particularly if it will make or break a potential contract.

In my opinion, companies should treat these services in the

same manner as they would when hiring security personnel. After all, if a regular employee has to go through a drug test and a criminal background check to be in your offices, why shouldn't a janitorial work crew have to do the same? They have greater access to offices, and all the confidential information in them, than any one employee might otherwise have.

Isn't it interesting that you would not expect to see a marketing department employee wandering inside the office of an executive in the finance department when that executive isn't there. Yet, a worker on the janitorial crew is more likely to have unquestioned access to all offices, in all departments, when no one is around. And if one of the regular crew members is out sick for a night, or on vacation for a week, a substitute steps in and gains the same access—even though your company knows absolutely nothing about this person. The same issues present themselves with temporary help in your office staff. What do you know of the background of a "temp" who fills in for your absent employee for anywhere from a day to weeks or months?

I can hear some people saying, "Let's be practical. How can we timely verify the background of a telephone service person, for example, who enters our premises to fix a phone on a one-time basis?" You can't. But what you can do in that situation is provide appropriate levels of physical security to oversee the service person. Someone (preferably, to avoid intimidation, not a uniformed officer, but a regular office person) should remain in the office where the phone is being repaired. At the same time, your security people should be sure there's no access to areas not relevant to the repair job at hand.

And while I don't want to make you paranoid over this, you should consider that a telephone service person can easily plant a bugging device on your phone to record all calls from a particular extension. By the way, if your confidential papers are handled as I've suggested, you could lessen the risk that repair persons, in the course of making repairs (or even a janitorial service crew), will glimpse information they're not supposed to see.

The point here is to be diligent on all fronts, not only for physical security, but for your computer-based and paper-file information as well. And if your service people are "regulars," it should be easier to require background reviews on each of them, to find out who they really are. As a condition of their working in your offices, you can obtain their consents to do an appropriate background check. In any event, though, don't ignore the security of locked file drawers and document-sanitized desktops.

Tapper's Tip #91

Verify the janitorial team's credentials the same as you would your own employees for hire, but be sure to observe all laws protecting privacy of personal information. Don't investigate a person's background without first obtaining their consent.

Wastebaskets or treasure troves?

There's much truth to the saying that "one man's trash is another man's treasure." This fact particularly applies to the papers you throw away on a daily basis. Your company's wastebaskets could contain highly confidential spreadsheet information, discarded customer lists that were downloaded as printouts, drafts of contracts, memos, and reports that may be outdated, but still confidential.

Tapper's Tip #92

Your wastebasket is a treasure trove for competitors. Don't feed the competition.

Tapper's Tip #93

With the low cost of shredders today, no office should be without one. In fact, each person who produces a fair amount of paper trash should have his own shredder. *If you're throwing it away, shred it today!*

There's no lack of cases involving companies who engage others to get the trash bags from competitors to examine their trash. It happened to Microsoft when one of its fiercest competitors engaged a corporate espionage firm to collect and rummage through its trash for correspondence and printouts that, they hoped, would show Microsoft made payments to certain organizations to obtain their support for Microsoft's defense in the government's antitrust case against it. The cleaning service empties your wastebaskets each night into large plastic bags, and those bags either get put out immediately for garbage collection, or taken away by the crew for later disposal. If your throw-away papers aren't shredded, they're all ready-to-read by whoever nabs your trash.

Courts have grappled with the question of when, and under what circumstances, your trash becomes public property. The outcome of these decisions has depended on the location of the court (in a state or federal court, for example) and the specific facts of the controversy, such as where the trash was stationed at the time it was taken away or rummaged through. If it's at the street side, the trash is more likely to be considered public property. But if it's still on your property, and a truck must drive into a loading dock area for pickup, there may be a strong argument the trash is private property until it's loaded onto the truck. Why place your company and its legal team in that predicament? You can control the outcome: shred it before it gets to the bag. It won't matter, then, who grabs it.

Copy Centers

Do you have copy centers inside your company? Is there a centralized place where volume copying and assembly of large reports take place? Companies have a tendency to hire less educated or less experienced workers for this area, thinking that the job is oriented on the mechanical side: operating the copier functions and applying skills in binding reports with various kinds of assembly materials. Keep in mind, though, that some of the most highly confidential material in your company may pass through their hands, visible to their eyes.

What controls do you have there? How easy is it for someone to collate and remove one additional report, when 30 or 40 are being done? What might happen to that "extra" report? Will you catch it? And what happens to the pages that don't turn out quite right? Are they shredded, or simply thrown away "whole" in the nearest wastebasket? During the time that a large and highly confidential report is being assembled, with papers spread all around, who else is allowed access to the room? What controls do you have to secure this activity?

Tapper's Tip #94

Be diligent in controlling, protecting, and managing confidential information at copy center operations, because laxity can cause your company to breach its contractual obligations to others, and lose protection for its trade secrets. Initiate audit procedures to assure compliance.

If you don't have a copy center in-house, do you farm out the project to a local copy center? If so, who are those employees at the center who will be handling your sensitive material? What do you know about them? Probably, very little. Did you ever think that if some are part-time workers, their full-time job could be at your competitor's company? You can be assured your company has no "non-disclosure" contract with any of these employees. What are their security procedures, if any? And what do you think will happen when you tell the person in charge that you want his service to protect your information because it's "highly confidential"? Very likely, you'll simply pique their curiosity for a closer look at what it is, and who knows what will happen to it afterwards? And how do you know how many additional "unbilled" copies will be made without your knowledge?

The solution to this is to adopt and enforce stringent security controls for your own in-house copying. Avoid using outside copy centers for copying sensitive and confidential information. Also be aware that if any of the copies you're making involve attorney-client communications—memos, reports, analyses, correspondence—you'll destroy their privileged nature by allowing a third party to see them. That, in itself, could prove harmful in future litigation.

In many instances, your company has contracted with outside consulting firms or other vendors on specific projects. Did your company agree to protect confidentiality of information acquired and exchanged mutually through the relationship? If so, when you give a store clerk at a copy center your consultant's private report to copy, you will, singlehandedly, breach the confidentiality terms of the agreement. And if any of the information is a "trade secret," you will destroy your company's ability to protect it later in court. A "secret" that's visible and accessible to a non-employee (such as a worker at your downtown copy center) is no longer a "secret."

Tapper's Tip #95

Don't farm-out confidential copying jobs to outside copy centers, unless you have the same protections for confidentiality that you would expect if they were done in-house. If that assurance isn't "air-tight," put your own people in charge of the copying.

Try going to your neighborhood copy center and asking the manager if she and her employees would sign a non-disclosure agreement for your company before taking on the job assignment.

Good luck!

Chapter 6

The Privacy Trap

Guarding your customers' personal data

Privacy. We all believe we're entitled to it. But, where the law is concerned, privacy is a lot more complicated than you might think. Politicians champion privacy rights for consumers while legislatures at state and federal levels pass new laws to guarantee them. And who do you think bears the burden of these laws? You do, if you're in a company that collects personal information from customers or clients.

Tapper's Tip #96

Warning! The difference between a company's public image of how careful it is in protecting its customers' privacy, and its actual "inside" practice, will be the next smoking gun in the trial lawyers' "gotcha" bag.

Retailers and institutions, such as banks and security brokerage firms, request and receive so much personal detail from their customers that their customer lists are not just names and addresses anymore. They're personal profiles that contain social security numbers, identity of bank accounts and balances, credit card numbers, spouses' names, anniversary dates, birth dates, names and ages of children, lists of assets and their values, and more.

When a company issues a new credit card or store card (it doesn't matter what kind, so long as it serves to identify the person through a swipe in a card reader), another paper trail begins. Every transaction is recorded, tracking the customer's purchases, and creating a profile on the customer's "value." The marketing staff, hoping to squeeze every bit of value out of this information, will use it to build a stronger, more loyalty-bound, and trusting relationship between company and customer. It's called "customer relationship marketing" (CRM).

Tapper's Tip #97

The bond between customer and company is one of trust, and a significant portion of that trust is the customer's reliance on the company to always "do right" by her. More than ever, "doing right" requires protecting the privacy of the personal information the customer "confides" to the company. Do whatever it takes to protect that trust, because the cost of keeping it is always less than the cost of losing it.

As the relationship develops, and the consumer continues to patronize your company's sales or services, the consumer leaves a paper trail that could become a double-edged sword. It can backfire on the consumer's personal life because it shows a "history" of his transactions, which may, or may not, be to his best interests. It could also subject the company that keeps recording the trail to liability if lax security practices expose the information to misuse by its own employees, affiliates, or third parties with whom it may share the information.

Let's see how this works, using an example from the casino entertainment environment. The casino entertainment industry provides a prime example of how CRM works with paper trails because casino companies are keenly focused on customer service and cultivation of customer loyalty. The "player identification" card is their essential relationship-building tool.

Consider yourself as the consumer, enjoying a night out at your favorite casino. Each casino encourages you to sign up for its free player card, which it uses to rate your frequency, and type, of play at the tables or slot machines. By using the card each time you play, you qualify for points that earn "free" services or products, called "comps." If you achieve the right number of points, you may qualify for a free hotel stay, a lunch or dinner at one of the casino's restaurants, or tickets to a live stage show. When you fill out an application you receive your player card right there, on the spot, and are rewarded with a few incentives that give you some instant "freebies."

When you insert your card into the slot machine, the microchip processor inside reads your identity, and begins recording all of the details of your play. Depending on the degree of sophistication of a casino's computer system, the data may include the exact time you started to play, how much coin you put into the machine, how much coin dropped out, your wins and losses, and the time you stopped playing, including the identification of the machine you played on. This information is stored on the casino's database, retrievable at any time for a printout of the "value" of your play for marketing purposes. CRM is in full operation here. When the casino evaluates your "trail," it takes steps to build and earn your loyalty by catering to what pleases you, as it determines your behavioral play and spending patterns.

This information is retrievable, typically, by authorized employees in marketing, the casino credit department, the casino host office, or other departments that have anything to do with CRM. By collecting this data, the company has assumed an enormous responsibility to see that your information is handled in a confidential manner, and not misused, or misappropriated, by unauthorized employees. Internal controls on accessing this information better be stringent. (Indeed, one casino company boasts that it has over 21 million customers in its combined database from all of its casino properties, nationwide.)

Tapper's Tip #98

If your company advertises the benefits of its customer database for customer service, it better spare no expense in adopting, and enforcing, the highest caliber security controls to protect and restrict access to the information. If your access controls are only on paper, you could be facing an inside risk of misuse, or misappropriation, by employees, or an outside risk of penetration by hackers, either one of which can cause a devastating loss.

As a consumer, you don't really think about the trail you've left behind. That is, not until you're involved in a lawsuit, such as a divorce, child or spousal support proceedings, or collection of a debt, and the plaintiff's lawyer subpoenas the casino for your records which, of course, include your paper trail. Divorce lawyers who seek judgments against spouses for support money, or alimony, often serve subpoenas on casinos for these records, wanting to know the spending activities of a spouse who dodges support payments and alleges inability to pay. The Internal Revenue Service also serves subpoenas for information about specific persons, including their gambling activities, credit profiles from credit applications, and approved casino credit limits. It's not unusual for a state's attorney general to seek similar evidence on individuals who may be the subject of criminal investigations for grand juries.

For the company served with these subpoenas, it's not a matter of choice to release or not to release the information. It's an obligation of the law. The only "choice" is to comply with the law and release the information. Otherwise, the company and its officers could be held in "contempt of court," subject to fines, and jail time for the officers.

Don't think this happens only at casinos. It occurs wherever you create a paper trail. With different details, it happens at hotels you stay in, airlines you travel on, and wherever else you use an "identifier," such as a credit card, debit card, frequent flyer card, or the like. Your credit card bills, aside from showing your indebtedness, have a wealth of information about you, with a paper trail that investigators can use to determine your buying habits, like the places you visited and used your card, the kinds of items purchased, and maybe, even the actual time of the purchase, in addition to the date. The receipts for these items can all be subpoenaed from the credit card companies by your adversary, if relevant to a lawsuit against you.

Any place you use an "identifier," and any record you make by giving out information about yourself, is discoverable. You've heard the saying, and it's true: "You can run, but you can't hide." Not so long as you use credit cards, or other identifiers, in the places you visit, or the things you apply for.

Your paper trail keeps getting longer. Just look at the trails you leave in public records, starting with motor vehicle registrations and drivers' license files, voter registration records, county real estate records that show what you paid for your house and who holds the mortgage, including all the terms of the mortgage. Then, there's the information in county records such as birth certificates, marriage certificates, death certificates, divorce records, arrest records, and more, on almost anyone you want to look up. The U.S. Postal Service even stands ready to give out your forwarding address when you move.

Not long ago, the U.S. Congress passed, and President Clinton signed into law, the Gramm-Leach-Bliley Act (GLBA), which governs financial institutions and their treatment of "nonpublic personal information" (information collected about the consumer in connection with the service or product the institution provides). The GLBA requires these institutions to send "Privacy Notices to Consumers." The Notice tells you how the institution uses your private information, and whether it shares any of it with so-called "non-affiliated third parties." These notices must be "clear and conspicuous," written in plain language, with an easily readable typestyle, and they must be accurate in what they represent as privacy practices.

A typical Privacy Notice contains language similar to this from a form, produced for banking institutions, by Bankers Systems, Inc., in St. Cloud, MN:

"We restrict access to nonpublic personal information about you to those employees who need to know that information to provide products or services to you. We maintain physical, electronic, and procedural safeguards that comply with federal standards to guard your nonpublic personal information."

If your company is subject to this federal law (as was the security brokerage firm I told you about in Chapter 5), you'll need to assure compliance. Those companies that want to stay out of the privacy traps should take steps to exceed the federal standards by applying extra precautions to protect the privacy of customers' information. If you show that your company not only meets, but exceeds, the standards, you will strengthen its defense position immensely in a breach of privacy suit. Even if your company is not subject to this specific federal law, it should still make itself aware of all other laws concerning consumer information privacy that pertain to its industry and its operations.

For institutions covered by the GLBA, the potential smoking gun (and privacy trap) is in the difference between what they represent in their privacy notices, and their actual practices. How your company measures up can be determined through an independent third party audit that checks the quality of your internal program for monitoring compliance, and the effectiveness of your programs to train employees how to handle this nonpublic, personal consumer information.

When the process server comes knocking at the company's door to deliver papers announcing the next lawsuit, you can be assured the plaintiff's lawyer will search for actual security practices in place, and compare them to the company's stated privacy policy. The effectiveness of your risk controls, particularly as to the clearance levels of employees who can access this information, will figure prominently in whether your company has smoking guns in its midst.

There are numerous other laws, state and federal, concerning some form of consumer privacy, and the company's obligation to protect it. The rules and regulations keep accumulating, and so do the company's responsibilities. You cannot, without dire consequences, ignore those burdens. Focus now on controlling and protecting the sanctity of all of this confidential information as an integral part of your company's operations. To do less is to endanger the lifeblood of your operations.

If your company has a significant presence in the world of e-commerce, it also faces the daunting challenge of staying ahead of hackers who try to infiltrate your databases and steal your customers' personal credit information. In December, 2000, Egghead.com, a technology products retailer, notified credit card companies, the FBI, and 3.5 million customers (its registered users) that a hacker had infiltrated its computer systems, and may have stolen its customers' credit information. This happened just days before Christmas, when the company knew its system had been violated, but couldn't tell, initially, what had been taken, if anything. As a precautionary move, they alerted their customers to be on the lookout for misuse of their cards during that busy holiday season. It turned out that other security measures in place prevented the downloading of the credit card information, but the company received some criticism for electronically storing customers' credit card numbers in the first place. Storage of customers' credit profiles on the website was a convenience the company provided so its customers could make future purchases without having to re-key their credit card information each time. (Egghead announced it would reconsider its policy as a result of the event, but later, the company went out of business, for reasons unrelated to this.)

Egghead wasn't alone in facing these attacks, and the consumers on the Internet are no closer to feeling more secure about giving their personal information to E-commerce companies. On March 5, 2001, Reuters Limited reported that hackers had, for several months' time, been downloading the credit card information stored on the servers of Bibliofind, an online bookseller. Another well known company, Western Union, closed its Web site for five days in September, 2000, after discovering that hackers stole an estimated 15,000 credit card numbers. And now, it's getting to be more of a common practice that e-commerce companies no longer make public announcements when hackers have attacked their websites. Apparently, the companies have assessed the risks and found that the extent of the security breaches and the damage done by them were not anything near the damage they'd face by a public announcement of the events. Once eroded, consumer confidence and trust are hard to regain. And don't forget the class action lawyers who are always circling overhead.

Failing to implement state-of-the-art security measures, though, with immediate urgency, is a "bet the company" risk. If consumers discover that you have no meaningful, and consistently enforced, controls for physical and technical access to your computer data, they'll take their business elsewhere.

It only takes one lawsuit where pretrial discovery exposes your lax or nonexistent security practices. The word leaks out to the media and a story is born. It may then be fueled by your own employees (at least some of the disgruntled or discontented ones) who seek an outlet through reporters on a nameless "sources within" basis. That's when your customer list will suffer a gross devaluation, and the class action hounds will be after you for a a potential punitive damage verdict on behalf of all customers whose information may have been mishandled.

It's a formidable price to pay because, at the retail level, the customer list (assuming it has been well-developed, and kept current) has a tremendous, competitive market value as a trade secret. Mergers and acquisitions are attractive, in many instances, for the sheer value of such an active list, with its ability to expand another company's market segment. This customer information is often the real heart of an acquisition deal, and the rest that comes with it is mere "icing on the cake."

How much of your company's resources are devoted to protecting this asset in the manner befitting its value? In the majority of cases, I can predict it's not enough.

Don't kid yourself by taking it for granted.

Chapter 7

Accessing Company Secrets

"Password" to gold

Do you have any idea how many people, and at what level, have daily access to the millions of pages of information on your computer systems? If you want the pulse rate of just how serious your company is in protecting its computer-based information, check the difficulty, or ease, of getting access to it. Access control is the heart of any serious computer security system, and as such, if it fails, your security fails.

The common way for a user to gain access to electronic information is through a "password." If it only takes a single password to obtain access to important proprietary data files, and there are no restrictions on whether a person's access is for "read-only," or "read-write" (which gives ability to delete or modify), your company is wide-open for fraudulent and malicious entries, or theft of data. Unauthorized users who gain knowledge of someone's password can not only read and copy sensitive personal data of customers, including financial information on bank accounts, credit cards, and social security numbers, but can delete information with a malicious intent. Most, if not all, of this activity will go undetected if you have no built-in audit trails that track a user's activity.

Any system of access control should consider creating levels of access based on an employee's job function. For example, some employees may function on a read-only level, while others may have authority to read and modify, and only a select few will have acess to read, write, and delete. On top of that, there should be certain informational levels that impose limits on the depth of material that's accessible. Highly confidential information should, itself, be encoded so it can't be opened as a file without the proper code, or password entry. Even at that, an employee should be required to enter an employee identifier for security clearance purposes. The system should also be designed to continually audit, and track, the current and past users.

So many systems have no checks and balances to protect privacy or access. The deficiencies center around PASSWORDS, the "keys" to access. For that reason, I'll show you how to strengthen that chain by looking at password problems that have been identified in company settings.

Tapper's Tip #99

Passwords are the "keys" to access, but they're also the weakest link in your data security chain, if not administered with strict oversight.

Disable passwords, immediately, of employees who leave

For those who are no longer associated with your company, do you have a consistent procedure for deleting, or disabling, their accounts and their passwords, immediately, on the date and hour they leave? With an overloaded workday, it's easy for that one person to forget to take the necessary action. If the person in charge is away on the day when an employee leaves, the matter may be left undone until she returns, and that should be unacceptable in any security system.

Tapper's Tip #100

Set up a system for immediate shut-down of passwords for employees who leave your company.

I've heard stories of companies that had such procedures in place, but they depended on one person to perform them, without any oversight. The departing person's passwords, voice-mail, and e-mail accounts remained active for weeks until someone brought it to the attention of Human Resources which, in turn, had to contact a Systems Administrator for telephones, and another one for computers, causing uncalled-for delays. Put procedures in place that don't depend on one person to administer. To "lock-out" an employee's password access, you should have programmed steps that authorized persons (with a password code) can follow to accomplish the task.

Limit passwords used by consultants

If you provide temporary passwords to outside consultants who work on maintenance or programming of your systems, does anyone monitor the period of their access? Do you limit access to a designated time? Who controls the deletion of the password when the consultant's job is done?

Consultants have special expertise in working their way through data files on your company's systems. Indeed, that's why you hire them. But that's also why you are particularly vulnerable if you don't have adequate measures in place to closely restrict the use of password access. Some consultants work from their offices, and access your computer system through modem connections. You should consider passwords that open only limited pathways, which allow only selective retrieval of information. If the consultant is working on changing mailing list operations, for example, why provide blanket access to company financial data, or other files that are unrelated?

Consultants have enough technical know-how to re-enter the company's system from remote locations after a job is completed. Unscrupulous consultants can use the information to their own advantage, or sell the access to a third party. Background and reputation play a significant role here, but that's still not a guarantee.

Prosecutors around the country have been tackling complaints of computer crimes with increasing frequency. In some states, up to one-third of those complaints are against computer consultants who had access to the company's computer systems. Traditional safeguards of background checks, and powerful, detailed clauses in consultant's contracts to protect the company against disclosure, or use, of secrets are helpful, but not foolproof.

Be sure to have your company's attorney include a "no-access" clause in a consultant's contract. This forbids the consultant from using any access to your systems at the moment the consultant leaves your premises, or if you prefer, at any time after the completion date of the specific project. Or, you can specify that at no time shall the system be accessed from remote sources.

Tapper's Tip #101

Provide special passwords with limited pathways for consultants who have access to your system, to reduce unnecessary electronic "sightseeing."

Alter passwords when job titles change

If an employee changes jobs within your company, does anyone review whether the new job function requires the same level of access as before? This is an easy one to overlook because of the comfort level of working with a familiar employee. However, there may be no reason why that person should have continued access at the prior clearance level.

Tapper's Tip #102

Security clearance levels should be reviewed when an employee's job function changes. Access should be consistent with new responsibilities.

Assign passwords only to those who need them

Are your managers exercising diligence in determining which people on their staffs actually need access to the data? You should be cautious in overseeing the laxity of managers who do not sense the need for restricted access and protection of company data. Don't let them hand out passwords, unnecessarily, to too many staffers.

Tapper's Tip #103

Managers should be trained in password security and admonished not to hand out passwords for staffers who have no access need.

Forbid the use of a common password formula

Does your company use common passwords with the employee's first name initial and last name, or the first and last names as "default" passwords? When a customized password is not chosen, many systems are designed to accept a "default" password. The problem is that everyone knows about them, so why use them? It's like locking the door to your home, then leaving the key under the doormat. Does that really give you any sense of security from unauthorized entry?

Tapper's Tip #104

Avoid using common configurations for passwords. They're no better for security than leaving your house key under the doormat.

Protect your password or it could come back to haunt

How many employees enter their passwords while their friends or colleagues are sitting or standing nearby? Keystrokes are easily seen, so you should use discretion on entering your password in front of others.

And when they can't be seen, it appears that they now can be recorded for replay at a later time. The Associated Press reported on 7/30/01, that the FBI has developed a bugging device that can record every keystroke on your keyboard. According to the report, the FBI had the son of a former Philadelphia mob boss under surveillance when they discovered that the e-mails he typed were encrypted with a password. Unable to decipher the e-mails without the password, they gained entry to his business, secretly placed the device on his computer, and recorded the keystrokes from his keyboard, revealing the password they needed. If this device ever becomes available in the commercial market, it could have a profound effect on the issue of personal privacy.

For employees, the danger of having someone else access the system by using your password is that you can be "framed," unsuspectingly, by a jealous or devious co-worker. (Although we mentioned this in Chapter 3, on e-mail smoking guns, it bears mentioning again.) Using your password, anyone with malicious motive can send a nasty e-mail to management through your e-mail account, and it will appear as if it came from you. Or more subtly, an e-mail can be sent from your account to another colleague, making derogatory references to management people, with a blind copy sent directly to a manager, supervisor, or officer. If there's an audit tracking system that tracks all users who download files, the person who improperly accessed your system may download certain files that are considered confidential, causing management to suspect wrongdoing on *your* part.

Don't allow passwords to change, without approval

Do you instruct employees on the shortcut steps on how to re-program their passwords so they can change them whenever they want? Avoid this vulnerability by requiring all passwords to be registered before use.

You can't effectively track users of your system when there's no control on registration of passwords. Keep in mind, though, that the registration list of passwords is, in itself, a highly confidential file, which must be protected at the highest security level. One person, though, should not have access to all of the registered passwords. The number of people with such access, and the clearance level those passwords can unlock, must be closely monitored. Passwords that enable the highest clearance levels in the company should be safeguarded at the key management level. When a person with access to a password registration list leaves the company, the appropriate exercise of caution is to immediately change all passwords on that list.

The company should retain records of all users' passwords, and the levels of clearance for each user, so that appropriate changes can be made as soon as any user leaves the company, or changes job title and responsibilities.

Tapper's Tip #106

Passwords should be centrally registered, and monitored, and the registration should be treated as you would a trade secret, with the highest level of security.

Beyond Passwords:
Additional security measures for access controls

If you adopt password precautions, your computer system will have far more security control. However, access controls include security measures beyond password issues, so your company should consider some, or all, of the following:

CONTROL THE ABILITY TO CHANGE APPLICATION PROGRAMS

The software programs you use for applications should have built-in restrictions against modification or deletion by anyone other than a highly skilled, and specifically authorized technician, with an assigned, and guarded, password entry. These controls should be designed to restrict computer consultants, who are usually called in as programmers, to fixing bugs and making modifications to customize programs. When you grant such access, don't forget the need to control the amount of depth of informational levels that the consultant can access. Restrict the person from wandering too deeply into your system, and "picking-off" information he doesn't need to see.

SEPARATE THE PROGRAMMING RESPONSIBILITIES TO AVOID ONE-PERSON CONTROL

When authorizing access levels for making program changes, it's a good idea not to place full authority in one person for writing, testing, and approving the program changes. It's best to have more than one person assigned to a project to perform different segments of the process. This lessens the risk of tampering, without detection, and avoids one-person control that could undermine the system.

SECURE YOUR OPERATING SYSTEM

Be careful that while you're protecting access to application programs, you don't neglect the security of the operating system. Anyone accessing the operating system's files should have "read-only" status, unless that person passes through built-in safeguards that require, at a minimum, verified identification as a user.

PLAN NOW FOR DISASTER AND AVOID LOSS OF DATA (WHILE DISCOVERING VULNERABILITY)

What controls are in place to meet emergency situations? Does your company have contingency plans to continue operations if there's a power failure? Do you have procedures for back-up of data? Hopefully, your back-up procedures will coincide with document retention policies, so you don't keep unnecessary archives of information in storage. What if some facilities on a network system go down? Do they interrupt service to the entire network? Is there an alternate way to get information to the service branches? Are you content to have your operation shut-down if computers go down?

If there is a contingency plan for emergencies, has it been tested? Have you done an assessment of where your critical operations take place? How will you replace them by alternate means if power goes out? Are your computer cables, modem lines, and data cable lines running under your flooring material? If so, what if you have a flood? Would a flood take your whole system out, or would it destroy sections of data operations? Do you have off-site backup computers that can be switched on in an emergency?

Just how much you want to spend on back-up and contingency plans, or as some refer to it, "disaster recovery plans," depends on how critical your computer system is to your operations. If your system were to go out, how long could you stay open for business without it?

I recently visited the U.S. Post Office to mail a package, and arrived there at 8:30 am, when the office was supposed to open. After a half-hour in line, a postal worker appeared through the glass front door, and yelled, "The computers are down, and we have someone at the central office working on the problem." The post office didn't open for business until 10:30 that morning.

The functions covered by computer were electronic scales that weighed a package, or letter, and determined the amount of postage for the different choices of services. Whatever happened to manual postal scales to weigh packages, instead of electronic ones? Or manual arithmetic, to add up postage amounts with pencil and paper, and make change for customers? What about the people who just wanted to buy some stamps? If the sales couldn't be recorded electronically, why couldn't they be entered later, from a hand-kept log, after the computers were up and running? Or, why couldn't the postal service switch its system, to link to the computer system of another post office branch, whose system was up and running? So much for contingency plans which, in this case, called for simple solutions.

Create a position for Chief Privacy Officer

The workplace today has so many issues concerning information management and protection, that it warrants creation of a full-time, high level, managerial position. This leadership position carries the title of Chief Privacy Officer, or "CPO, " and will focus on protecting confidential information in the workplace, protecting the privacy of customers' personal credit information, adoption of e-mail policies and Internet usage policies, and diligent management and coordination of access controls to electronic information.

This office differs from a Chief of Information Technology whose job is, usually, more related to systems and programming, technical operations, equipment upkeep, and fulfillment of company objectives through technology. The CPO's focus is more concentrated on issues of privacy, and protection of content of data of every kind, regardless of form.

A basic functional job description for a CPO may go something like this:

Chief Privacy Officer (CPO)

♦ Plans and develops policies to enforce effective safeguards that protect the privacy and integrity of informational storage and retrieval company-wide.

♦ Monitors, tests, and evaluates the effectiveness of controls.

♦ Analyzes and evaluates work flow and communication distribution needs on employee, departmental, and divisional levels.

♦ Implements consistent audit controls for all information, electronic and paper, to preserve confidentiality of selected material.

♦ Initiates risk management procedures to reduce vulnerability of access to confidential information, including separation of duties and responsibilities among authorized access users, in an audit system with checks-and-balances.

♦ Establishes appropriate procedures and policies for identification, labeling, and handling of all intellectual property, which includes patents, licenses, and related information, copyrights, trade secrets, and any other information determined to be confidential, or of a nature requiring restricted access.

♦ Drafts, with assistance of counsel, effective document retention policies, e-mail and Internet usage policies, electronic retention policies, and implements them; monitors compliance to the policies and procedures and enforces them in a uniform and consistent manner.

♦ Verifies backgrounds of every outsider that has any "inside" business with the company, or that has, or will be granted, access to the company's facilities.

The person who fills this position should have key management authority, with a clear understanding of the technology of your company's electronic information systems. Beyond that, the

CPO must be a well-organized person, demonstrate effective leadership ability, and demonstrate a management style that gets people motivated. Ideally, this person will also have working knowledge of the laws governing privacy and confidentiality, and be capable of effectively translating them into active, and practical, policies that are consistently enforced.

Above all, there's no room here for mediocrity.

Chapter 8

The Attorney-Client Privileged Communication

Last bastion of secrecy

Almost everything you say, do, or write in the workplace is fair game for disclosure in litigation, and what a thin line you walk in maintaining "confidentiality." The last bastion for protection from disclosure is the "attorney-client privileged communication."

If you have the right ingredients to create such a communication, whether it's through a conversation, e-mail, voice mail, file on floppy disk, or letter, memo, report, or tape recording—the form doesn't matter—the law will cloak the communication with a privilege to keep its contents from disclosure to anyone, at anytime, forever. "Forever" means until any party to the communication intentionally gives it up, or inadvertently slips up, on the rules to maintain it.

Tapper's Tip #107

If you're ever on the receiving end of a confidential conversation, memo, e-mail, or report, intended to be cloaked with the protection of an attorney-client privileged communication, you owe it to yourself, and your company, to know the rules to protect the privilege, as well as the pitfalls that can trap you into losing it.

The last thing you want is your company pointing to you as the reason for having to turn over a controversial document to the opposing lawyers—one that it expected would be protected as an attorney-client privileged communication. In this chapter, you'll find what it takes to create an attorney-client communication, what the "privilege" means, and what you need to know so you don't destroy it unintentionally.

Test Your Perceptions

Recent surveys of management people in large and small companies reveal that company managers mistakenly think they know more than they do about how the attorney-client privilege works. Their "knowledge" is filled with misconceptions that pervade the ranks, from top management on down. Even in-house attorneys who have no prior litigation experience, can fall victim to these same misconceptions.

For example, test your responses to the following questions:

Do you think:

> every communication you have with your company's attorney is "privileged"?

> that if an attorney sends you a memo marked "confidential" and "attorney-client privileged" that's enough to make it so?

> the information you give to company attorneys who investigate incidents in the workplace (whether for a sexual harassment claim, or to determine if employees have violated a company policy), is protected from future disclosure?

> that if the company's President assigns an in-house attorney to negotiate contracts, the negotiations and discussions leading up to the finalized contract, will be protected from future disclosure?

> that if you receive a memo marked "confidential" from your attorney, then make copies, and forward them to several other people for their comments, or for their information, the memo will still be a "privileged communication"?

> your company, in merger discussions with another company, can share attorney-client privileged documents with the acquirer's due diligence teams, without risking the loss of the privilege?

If you answered "yes" to any of these questions your perception is faulty. Read on to get the inside scoop. You need to know this stuff if you want to keep your words out of court, and the "confidence" in your confidential communications with attorneys intact.

How is this "privilege"created?

It takes three basic ingredients to create the attorney-client privilege. You must have the 1-2-3 to make it work:

(1.) *A communication between an attorney and client,*
(2.) *that is made in confidence, and*
(3.) *for the purpose of getting (as the client) or giving (as the attorney) legal advice or assistance.*

1. A communication between an attorney and client:

Your communication must be with an attorney. The method or manner of the communication doesn't matter much, whether it's in the form of a telephone call, a face-to-face conversation, an e-mail message, letter, note, memo, report, voice mail, recording, or other means of giving or getting a message to the attorney. It doesn't matter whether you or your attorney initiates the communication.

The privilege attaches to your communications with your attorney from the moment you start talking to him for the purpose of obtaining legal advice, whether or not the attorney decides to represent you. It doesn't matter, either, if your discussions are about anticipating a lawsuit, or seeking general legal advice, or needing representation because you want to sue somebody, or are being sued. The "communication" will still be privileged if it satisfies the other elements.

It's a little more complicated, though, when the company is the "client." When there are so many people in a company, who can we say speaks for the company as the "client"? As we would expect, the courts have tackled that issue on many occasions. Generally, any person in the "control group" can do so, which usually includes officers and key managers who have a substantial role in the decision-making process of the company. In the federal courts, the "control group" also includes any employee who is "sufficiently identified with the corporation," and this means managers, supervisors, and any others who have any kind of authority that enables them to speak for, or on behalf of, the company, even if it's only in their own division or department.

Tapper's Tip #108

If you have a supervisory function in the company, and an issue arises where you need legal advice to help you in the course of carrying out your duties, your communication with the company's attorney can qualify for the attorney-client privilege, on behalf of the company as the client.

In a partnership, the partners speak for the partnership. A person with the duties and responsibilities of a general manager, or anyone involved in key management decisions for the partnership, would also be capable of creating an attorney-client privileged communication for the partnership.

2. That is made in confidence:

The communication must be made "in confidence." You must intend that the exchange between you and the attorney be confidential. This means that no one outside of the attorney-client relationship is allowed to see a writing between you, or hear your conversation, or be told of the details of either.

Tapper's Tip #109

Don't tell anyone about the content of your communication with your attorney, or you will destroy its privileged status. In an individual client setting, if you bring a friend to your attorney's office to sit with you while you discuss matters with the attorney, the conversation loses its privileged status, because your friend is not a "client." In the corporate setting, those who are sufficiently identified with the company may be present if they each have a "need to know," on behalf of the company. Otherwise, the company risks losing the protection of non-disclosure.

Both the attorney and the client must protect confidentiality to maintain the privilege of non-disclosure. This makes sense, for if the content of the communication is no longer confidential between the client and the attorney, there's no reason to keep it from others. The law protects the "secrecy" of the exchange between the attorney and the client, so long as no one else (who isn't a "client") shares in, or is told about, the exchange. Once you breach the confidentiality requirement, the privilege is gone, lost forever for that communication.

It's fair to question that if you uphold your responsibility to keep the "confidence," what about the attorney's obligation? Be assured that there's nothing more sacred to an attorney than protecting and upholding the "privilege" of the communication with the client. It goes to the very core of the professional relationship between an attorney and a client. Not only is an attorney subject to liability for breaching that privilege, but an attorney can be disbarred for doing so, and there are very few attorneys who would ever risk that consequence.

Also, the law considers the client as "owning" the privilege, and only the client can give it up. That doesn't mean you can't authorize your attorney to "waive" it, because you can. Your attorney will assert and protect the privilege whenever the occasion threatens it (such as when another attorney questions you in a deposition and asks you what you said to your attorney on a particular occasion). But ultimately, you, or someone in your company (if your company is the client), controls the decision to disclose it.

That's not to say that sometimes, inadvertently, lawyers can't cause the privilege to be lost through casual conversations at dinner gatherings, conventions, and through cell phone and public phone conversations that are loud enough to be overheard by people nearby. But let's hope this is the exception, not the rule. You, too, should be circumspect when conversing with your lawyer in non-private environments, and while using technology that lacks security for privacy.

3. *For the purpose of getting (as the client) or giving (as the attorney) legal advice or assistance:*

This is, perhaps, the most misunderstood part of the requirements, and the one fraught with the most traps in the corporate setting. Your communication to the attorney must be for the purpose of getting *legal advice or legal assistance.* The attorney's communication to you must be for that purpose, and it's only that portion of the communication that deals with such purpose that's privileged. To obtain legal advice or legal assistance, you have to be seeking help that only an attorney is qualified to provide because of the attorney's knowledge and experience in the law.

The reason this requirement is easily breached in the corporate setting is because of the dual function served by an in-house attorney, who is not only a legal advisor to management, but a business advisor, too. Any communication from the attorney that can be construed as "business" advice will not qualify as a privileged communication. Although many executives think their communications on business subjects are protected from disclosure because they are conversing with an attorney, they're mistaken. When a company its in-house attorneys as part of the business team, the communications involving the attorney are likely to have no greater protection than any other "confidential" memo or report between managers.

Tapper's Tip #110

The only kind of communication between an attorney and client that qualifies as a privileged one requires, as its purpose, the getting, or giving, of legal advice or legal assistance. Any other matters in which you involve your counsel may be held "in confidence," but that doesn't mean they're privileged. And when they're not privileged, that makes them all discoverable in the pre-trial discovery stage of litigation.

The mere fact that you receive reports or memos from attorneys inside your company's law department, with a stamp at the top asserting "Attorney-Client Privileged Communication" doesn't make it so. But if you're not an attorney, you shouldn't make your own judgment as to whether it does or doesn't qualify for that status.

Always protect the communication, anyway, assuming it does, indeed, qualify. Do your part in upholding its confidentiality, and let the law department worry about future challenges to its privileged status. Their job will be easier if you follow their intentions. They won't take kindly to losing a battle over upholding its privileged status, when that loss is because of your lax handling of the "confidentiality" requirement.

What does this "privilege" really mean?

The "privilege" gives you the right to refuse to disclose what you actually say to your attorney, and what the attorney says to you, in response. That means you can refuse to testify about it, refuse to produce a copy of it, and refuse to answer any questions pertaining to it. Not even a grand jury, or a subpoena to testify, can make you disclose it.

Now, for the limitation: It does not protect you from having to disclose "facts" that you know, even if they were part of the attorney-client communication. For example, if you're asked the question, "Did you talk to your attorney?" you would have to answer "yes" or "no." But if you were asked, "What did you tell your attorney?" or "What did he tell you?" you could refuse to answer based on the attorney-client privilege. The other side has no right to know that information.

However, the opposing attorney can ask you (and you would be compelled to answer) specific questions directed to facts that you know about the issues in the case. The questioner doesn't actually know if you told this information to your attorney. His questions are directed to the facts, not to whether you told those facts to your attorney.

The point is you cannot shield facts from disclosure merely by telling them to your attorney, or sending a volume of papers containing those facts to him. Your attorney is not a closet to hide what otherwise can be discovered as part of normal pre-trial discovery rules in litigation.

Let's use an example and suppose there's a lawsuit by a female, former employee against your company, alleging sexual harassment as a result of suggestive cartoons that her supervisor (a male) posted on a bulletin board, and sent to her by e-mail. The supervisor meets with the company's attorney and discusses the facts of what occurred, and talks about the cartoons, the e-mails, and the relationship with the former employee. At the supervisor's deposition, the plaintiff's attorney asks him to name every instance in which he posted or sent a cartoon to the former employee, and to describe the contents of each cartoon. Just because he discussed this information with the company's attorney, beforehand, does not provide him with a shield for non-disclosure now. So long as the question does not ask what he actually said to the company's attorney, or what the attorney said to him, the privilege does not protect the factual information, within his personal knowledge, about an incident or event.

Why does our court system allow this privilege?

The privilege was created to encourage open, and frank, conversations between an attorney and client. The theory is that when a client knows that what she says will remain a secret, and the attorney she tells it to is ethics-bound to honor that secrecy, the exchange of information between attorney and client will flow more freely and truthfully. This is supposed to enable the attorney to give more accurate legal advice on the totality of facts, not just half-truths from a client holding back on them. Remember, that's the theory, even though it doesn't quite work like that in the real world.

More often than we'd like to remember, the client (and it doesn't matter if it's an individual, or a company, acting through its managers) will blind-side the attorney, and not tell him "everything." Sometimes, it's because the client didn't think the information was important, or he's afraid of the consequences if the information shows fault on his part. Unfortunately, the company's attorney usually discovers this in an embarrassing moment, during the deposition of a company officer, when the opposing attorney displays a memo or other document the company's attorney never saw before, revealing a whole slew of "new" facts that have the officer participating in much more of the activity in dispute than was previously known. And all of this now contradicts the foundation for the company's defense position. That's the time when the attorney deserves to take his client for a trip to the wood-shed.

Tapper's Tip #111

There are certain things, however, you might say to your attorney that releases the attorney from the ethical obligation to maintain secrecy, such as announcing your intentions to commit a crime or fraud upon others. Social policy dictates that it's more beneficial to prevent others from becoming victims of crime than to maintain the secret of a person about to become a criminal.

The "privilege" is actually a rule of evidence that's binding during pre-trial discovery, and the trial, itself. When a party invokes it to prevent disclosure of evidence, and the other side challenges your entitlement to the protection, the trial judge makes the ultimate decision as to whether your communication meets the 1-2-3 requirements.

Can you rely on the court upholding the privilege?

Short answer: No. Courts always have a tough decision when one side challenges the privilege, because it requires a careful balancing act between the positive social effects of two seemingly contradictory policies. One is the need to foster open, and honest, communication between an attorney and client and, thereby, protect those communications from disclosure. The other is the strong public policy of assuring full and fair discovery of all available evidence for trial ("the whole truth and nothing but the truth"). Although courts are respectful of the attorney-client privilege, they tend to be strictly conservative in reviewing a claim of privilege. If there's a weakness in any of the prerequisites to qualify for it (the "1-2-3" above), the courts will declare the privilege "waived," and require disclosure of the communication.

To prevent either side in litigation from taking unfair advantage of the other, by secreting evidence under the guise of "privilege," the rules require that whoever claims it must provide the other side with a "log," a list of the communications for which it's claimed. The log has to contain enough details for your opponent to determine if a challenge is worthy, while still allowing you to preserve the sanctity of the confidential information. It usually shows the date of each communication, the names of the parties to it, the people who were copied on it, a brief or generic description of the topic, such as "real estate matters," "marketing questions," or "regulatory inquiries," and the nature of the communication, such as "advice," "analysis," or "letter requesting advice."

If your side loses its claim of privilege, it's almost always a setback for your legal team. The defense regroups, and enters "damage control" mode to re-focus attention on how to combat the effects of disclosing the information contained in the formerly privileged communication.

The Company Setting: Privilege In Danger!

As I mentioned earlier, the task of preserving the attorney-client privilege in the corporate setting is formidable because the in-house attorney wears both a business hat, and a legal hat. In-house attorneys are active participants in business operations, including marketing, brand operations, public relations, strategic planning committees, audit committees, customer service operations, and risk management departments. Although they do give legal advice on issues as they arise, a lot of the discussions they participate in are business-focused, and don't require legal expertise, so much as good business judgment.

In a recent survey of CEO's of major public corporations, conducted by the professional trade magazine, *Corporate Counsel*, the CEO's were asked what they considered the most important skill of an in-house general counsel. The majority ranked the ability to perform as a "business lawyer" above performance as a "legal technician." In the eyes of a CEO, the value of an in-house counsel is in the business advice that counsel brings to the table.

The line between business advice and legal advice often gets shaded, and difficult to see, and that's where the challenge is. When an in-house attorney participates in a business meeting, and offers advice, it's sometimes impossible for an attorney to turn off all legal experience when thinking about solutions to business problems, and making suggestions for business plans or strategies. Because the foundational footing of an attorney-client privileged communication relies on an attorney giving legal advice, when the attorney's communication teeters between business and legal, the danger of losing the benefit of the privilege looms overhead. In-house attorneys err, in my opinion, when they confer with management through detailed, and frank discussions via e-mails or paper memos, taking for granted, to their and the company's detriment, that the contents of these communications will be protected from disclosure.

An opposing attorney will try to get the e-mail, memo, or other document by challenging the company's claim of privilege, asserting that business advice was the primary purpose of the communication. To assess if the document will survive the challenge, you'll need to do what a court would do: look closely at the overall intent and purpose of the communication, and determine if the attorney who authored it distinguishes the business advice from the legal advice. If the distinction isn't obvious, determine if the tone and content are more "business-oriented," as opposed to "legal-oriented."

If you want more assurance that the communication will be cloaked with the protection of the privilege, separate your request for business advice from legal advice more distinctly, and have your attorney respond in the same way.

Tapper's Tip #112

When you ask the company's in-house attorney for advice, you should distinguish whether it's "legal advice," or "business advice," you want. If the response combines both, it may lose the protection of a privileged communication, if it's difficult to tell where the business advice ends, and the legal advice begins.

Don't address a memo that includes a request for legal advice to anyone other than the attorney (and don't copy anyone else who is not part of the inner circle of "need to know" people on the issue). The more people (non-lawyers) to whom you circulate the request for advice, the more it becomes a business memorandum, instead of an attorney-client communication. If it's not a request for advice, but a statement of a new business proposal, for example, and you address it to a whole group of management with a copy to the company's attorney asking for comments from the recipients, that, too, is more inclined to be considered business correspondence rather than an attorney-client communication.

Breaking the Confidence

When you get an e-mail or memo from your company's attorney, don't forward it to a list of others who you think should see what counsel has to say, as that may instantly destroy the confidentiality requirement. Although the law will allow you to share the communication with a tight inner circle of people in the company who have a "need to know" the information in the message, you must tread carefully, as the "need" will depend on their participation and active involvement in the subject matter, and their responsibilities in the company. If your company's attorney has not included these people as additional addressees on the e-mail or memo, there may be a specific reason for this. Don't second-guess it; call the attorney who authored the e-mail or memo, and find out.

Tapper's Tip #113

When you get a letter or memo from the company's attorney, and it purports to be an attorney-client privileged communication, don't ever forward it to anyone else, or copy and show it to others, without permission from the attorney, or you'll risk destroying the privilege that attaches to it for non-disclosure.

Nothing is more disconcerting to an in-house counsel during the pre-trial discovery phase of litigation than to find that copies of his memo, addressed specifically to one or two particular officers as a "Confidential: Attorney-Client Privileged Communication," turn up in the separate files of several other employees or managers. And if that's not enough, the copies will usually include written notations in their margins from the person who "forwarded" a copy to the others! It's even more disturbing to find that one of those persons faxed a copy to an outside consultant who was working with him on the project.

Not only does the indiscriminate forwarding of copies of the "confidential" memo destroy the privilege, but all of the marginal notations are now discoverable as potential smoking guns.

Once you "open the gate," you invite opposing counsel down a new paper trail.

Chapter 9

Crisis Management

When it all "hits the fan"

How would your company, or organization, respond to the media, if it found itself in these front page events?

Hotel balcony collapses leaving 144 dead

Two suspended balcony walkways collapse while crowded with people during a tea-dance party at the Hyatt Regency Hotel in Kansas City, Mo., killing 144 people and leaving more than 200 others injured.

Exxon's oil tanker ruptures in Prince William Sound

The oil tanker Exxon Valdez strikes a barrier reef off the shores of Alaska in the Prince William Sound, spilling 11 million gallons of crude oil from its ruptured hull, which some called the worst environmental disaster in U.S. history.

E-coli contaminated burgers kill 4 kids, sicken 700 others at Jack-in-the-Box

Four children die and 700 other people fall ill from E-coli bacterial contamination after eating undercooked hamburgers from the Jack-in-the-Box restaurant chain in the northwestern area of the U.S.

EEOC files suit suit against Mitsubishi claiming pattern of sexual harassment of female workers

The Equal Employment Opportunity Commission (EEOC) filed a sexual harassment suit against Mitsubishi on behalf of hundreds of female workers at Mitsubishi's assembly plant in Normal, IL. Charging the company with a pattern of sexual discrimination that had allegedly been going on for years, the allegations included sexual assaults, degrading name-calling by male workers, and retaliation for complaints to supervisors.

Annual bonfire construction collapses at Texas A&M killing 12 students, injuring 27 more

Twelve college students die at Texas A & M University, and 27 others are injured, when a bonfire log stack, four-stories high, collapses during construction, burying or trapping most of its victims in the wooden avalanche. Victims' families seek answers from college officials who sanctioned and supervised the activity, while questions of student drinking and blood alcohol levels are probed by investigators.

Explosive stories! Yet, they're just a sampling of events that catapult companies into headline news. When the story tells of dead or injured people, and it points to your company's negligence, or its defective or contaminated product, as the cause, the outcome for the responsible party is CRISIS! Your company erupts with a compelling need for a public relations response, and answers and solutions that satisfy the public's and media's sense of fairness and accountability.

How a company responds to a crisis—its preparedness for "crisis management"—will define its public image and confirm, or destroy, its customers' loyalty and trust. If it makes the wrong moves, the suspicions created by not "telling it straight" will cause new and independent investigations, regulatory probes into the files, interviews with company employees, and the ultimate search for smoking guns.

Are you and your company prepared for managing the public relations that will get you through a crisis without devastating repercussions? Too many companies "think" they can handle it without much preparation, only to find, too late, how their lack of preparedness for this critical level backfires. Make no mistake here. This is where you'll most likely find your "weakest link" in the chain of skills for crisis management.

We know crisis management includes much more than public relations. It requires an assessment of the company's vulnerabilities, adoption of contingency plans to continue operations if a natural or man-made disaster occurs, the planning and implementation of risk management policies, and the training of a crisis response team to manage the process. Your company should invest the time and energy now to assure its preparedness for all facets of a crisis, and it shouldn't hesitate to hire the best experts in the field. This is one area that needs advance preparation; it's not a "wing-it" operation.

But for our purpose, we're going to focus on the public relations level, as it pertains to crises involving your company's product, or the negligence of those who supervise your operations. That's where you'll be treading across loaded minefields, and a misstep can trigger one explosion, which sets off another, in a

chain reaction that will drill you into a downward spiral. How
you avoid making the wrong moves at this critical level can best
be gleaned from studying examples of how other companies fared
in the court of public opinion, as they suffered their way through
real-time crisis management. We only really need two—the best,
and the worst.

Tapper's Tip #114

From studies done by experts, most of the companies that experience crises involving product liability or negligence knew,
or should have known, well in advance of their occurrence. The
issues that cause a crisis are usually simmering in a slow-boiling
pot that management keeps putting on the back burner, until the
day the pot boils over, spewing its "surprises."

What we'll see from the examples is that all the while the
pot is on the back burner, management unwittingly creates a
paper trail of memos, correspondence, analyses, reports, and
confidential documents that will likely become their smoking
guns when a crisis exposes these documents to lawyers, investigators, and the public.

When a company's allegedly defective product, or an
employee's negligent actions, affect the public's health and welfare, and the number of people affected keeps growing, a media
event is inevitable. What your officers and spokespeople say and
do, in response, will grab the public's attention, sending a story
instantly to the world through the news media, Internet, Web
sites, and chat rooms. And don't forget that, during this time,
plaintiffs' lawyers will have the company in the crosshairs of their
hunting scopes.

All it takes is one lawsuit that "smokes" out internal documents, either showing company officials had information, and opportunities, that could have prevented the present crisis, or revealing that the company's press releases have been false. When that information is leaked to the media, you'd better be ready to jump into the race to seize control of your PR, before the media and pundits have their field day speculating and reaching their own conclusions.

As the facts are unveiled, the public wants nothing but the "truth" about how, and why, the crisis happened. If it's a product liability issue causing injuries and deaths, they want to protect themselves and their families from falling victim to life-threatening consequences. And even if it's not, they're always deciding if their continued faith or trust in the company, and its brand, is well-placed.

People place more reliance on what is revealed in the company's internal documents, not intended for public disclosure, because they perceive them as "the true story," written in the private offices of executives when their guards were down, instead of through the sanitized and filtered scripts of the company's lawyers. After all, the internal documents usually bear a large red stamp at the top that says "CONFIDENTIAL," and that adds an aura of intrigue to outsiders, curious to get a chance to read what they weren't supposed to see.

Despite good intentions, without a carefully selected, trained, and skilled spokesperson as a communicator, people may not hear "integrity," "trust," and "sincerity" in the company's messages. Instead, they may associate "arrogance" with the company line, and think "smugness," "insincerity," and "profits first." Your company risks a public backlash when its message doesn't get through. How your message comes across makes all the difference between a public perception of stonewalling, or an image of integrity, and concern for the safety and welfare of your audience. You can't afford to have your message backfire.

It's time now to present the best and the worst of crisis

management case studies. (In the chapter following this, I'll provide you with the tips, techniques, and strategies that will strengthen the foundation of your own public relations level of crisis management.) Our two real-life examples are Johnson & Johnson's handling of its Tylenol product-tampering incidents of 1982, applauded as the best crisis management model in retail marketing history, and the Bridgestone/Firestone, Inc. tire recall of August, 2000, considered by many, as history's recent example of the worst.

The Tylenol Product-Tampering Incidents

It's the fall of 1982. Seven people in the Chicago area die unexpectedly and mysteriously. One is a twelve year-old girl who awoke during the night from discomforting cold symptoms. Her parents gave her an Extra-Strength Tylenol capsule to make her feel better. Comforted by the notion that the medicine would soon bring her relief, her parents went back to bed. By the time they awoke the next morning, their daughter was dead. In another part of town, a 27 year-old man took an Extra-Strength Tylenol capsule to relieve his minor chest pain. An hour later, his heart stopped, bringing sudden death. Grieving relatives rushed to his house. Among them were his brother and sister-in-law. They both developed headaches from all the trauma, and as they were unaware of what caused their relative's death, they went to the medicine cabinet and took an Extra-Strength Tylenol capsule apiece. Within two days, they, too, were dead.

Officials were puzzled over these deaths so close together, and in the same geographical vicinity. The breakthrough came when someone discovered that Extra-Strength Tylenol capsules were a common thread in the incidents. A quick analysis of the remaining capsules from the used containers at each victim's home revealed that the capsules had been laced with cyanide, a deadly poison. The amount stuffed in each capsule was 10,000 times more than needed for lethal effect.

Faced with a deadly crime of product-tampering, law enforcement authorities went into action, but the case to this day is still unsolved. As with all such cases, the reporting of the facts stimulated copycat crimes, and the tampering started spreading to other areas. Police went through Chicago neighborhoods warning of the danger. Network news broadcasts told the stories of deaths from "poisonous Tylenol." The Food and Drug Administration issued warnings to consumers not to use Tylenol in capsule form. The future of Tylenol, as an effective pain reliever, appeared doomed nationwide.

McNeil Consumer Products, a subsidiary of Johnson & Johnson, in New Brunswick, New Jersey, makers of Tylenol and many other health and medical products, had a nightmare on their hands. Their most profitable over-the-counter medicine was lethal. How could they restore the trust of their consumers? Who would ever want to ingest a Tylenol capsule again? Who would chance giving it to loved ones and take the responsibility for the consequences? Experts in marketing predicted the sudden death of the Tylenol brand. "No way they could survive this," said the pundits.

Johnson & Johnson responded in a manner that has now become the classroom model for teaching the best of crisis management. Immediately, the company's spokesperson took control, stepped in front of the cameras, and told the nation to stop using any type of Tylenol product until the investigation was completed to determine if the tampering was limited to one product and one locale, or was more widespread.

The company associated itself with investigative agencies in tracking down the perpetrators of the crime. It reached out to cooperate with, and sought the assistance of authorities, such as the Chicago Police, the FBI, and the Food and Drug Administration, and offered a $100,000. reward for information leading to the arrest and conviction of the killer. Its response made it clear the first concern was to insure the continued safety of the public, and their cooperation in sharing information with authorities, as well as the news media, confirmed it. The media organizations applauded the "nothing to hide" attitude of Johnson & Johnson and its subsidiary. The company was seen as much a victim as were the consumers.

Instead of trying to limit its damages and costs to a localized recall in the region where the incidents happened, the company decisively eliminated the widespread fear and concern for whether capsules anywhere else could have been tainted. It halted all production and advertising for Tylenol, and pulled all of the Tylenol capsules off the shelves, everywhere in the market—over 31 million containers, with a retail value of 100 million dollars. No law required the company to widen the recall beyond the production lots affected, or beyond the geographical region of the incidents. After all, there was no evidence of tampering with the product anywhere else.

As a lawyer, I can appreciate those who might view the response with a cynical perspective. By removing the entire capsule line from the market, the company avoided potential lawsuits if tainted capsules were found anywhere else in the country. After the company was obviously "on notice" of a problem with its product, if it didn't take prudent action to assure the product wasn't tainted in other areas of the country, plaintiffs might have successfully claimed that management was negligent for that failure. The recall was, therefore, not only an effective marketing success (because of the next phase of the crisis management that was underway), but a strategic risk management initiative. The motivation for action isn't as important as the end result, and benefit, to the consuming public. Whatever drove the company to its actions, the fact still remains that the company made the right moves to protect the public and preserve the integrity of its Tylenol product line.

In 1982, tamper-resistant packaging was unheard of in the marketplace. If the packaging didn't reveal evidence of tampering, how would a consumer know if poisonous capsules were substituted for the real thing? Other than change of color, or shape, or obvious marks that raised suspicion, you couldn't tell if someone else had opened the container. Therefore, when the company wiped out all of the existing product and eliminated second-guessing each time a consumer opened the container to take a capsule, it was hailed as a generous and noble move. The company's removal of all existing product ended the anxiety— an astute recognition of psychology's role in marketing.

Then, the company launched a brilliant marketing plan to restore the brand to its prominent position in the pain-reliever market. It re-introduced Tylenol capsules in triple-seal, tamper-resistant, packaging, and had the product on the shelves of retailers by December, that same year. They provided coupon incentives toward the purchase of any Tylenol product in addition to heavy discounts on all of its other products. A new advertising program emphasized how all other Tylenol products would also be manufactured, from then on, with the same tamper-resistant packaging. Johnson & Johnson led the industry, and everyone followed.

The comeback was a huge success, spurred mostly by the prompt response the company made to "get out in front" of the issues at the initial stage of the crisis, and adopt solutions that alleviated the fears of the public.

Tapper's Tip #115

Keeping in touch with the public, and their perception of events, is a key to good crisis management.

The company received millions of dollars' worth of "free" advertising through thousands of articles published around the world, in journals, magazines, and newspapers, praising not only the handling of the crisis, but the new packaging methods.

Good public relations kept the news media on their side. Some critics may say that crisis management wasn't too difficult, in this case, because the company was not fighting its own demons (smoking guns), while dealing with the main crisis. There's some validity to that, but the company still faced a situation that could have wiped out its leading product. Adept handling of public relations not only saved the day for it, but brought the product back stronger than ever, and changed an industry, and the public's expectations, for tamper-resistant packaging.

If your public relations activities are managed with precision and professionalism, you will arouse less suspicion of a smoking gun behind the main issue. The public relations level of crisis management is, therefore, a crucial link in overcoming the effects of adverse information from inside your company's files (paper or electronic).

To see how public relations is such a critical component when your company's crisis is combined with smoking guns, let's contrast the Johnson & Johnson example with that of Bridgestone/Firestone, Inc., and Ford Motor Company, in the August, 2000, tire recall crisis.

The Bridgestone/Firestone, Inc. and Ford Tire Recall

In the year 2000, Bridgestone/Firestone was the world's second largest tire maker, after Michelin. The tire brand had a 100-year-old history that instilled trust, and reflected "quality." Ford Motor Company, as one of the Big Three auto makers, embraced Firestone as a close contracting partner for that same period, and equipped its best-selling sport utility vehicles, the Ford Explorer and Mercury Mountaineer, with Firestone tires, including the ill-fated models that were later recalled.

Before Firestone announced what was to be the largest tire recall in history on August 9, 2000, evidence of "smoking guns" was surfacing almost daily in the media. Firestone fit the textbook example of companies that "brew" the issues on their back burners, long before their pots boil over.

By early 1999, reports showed that Ford was getting a volume of complaints from dealers in Saudi Arabia and neighboring nations about wrecks involving its Explorer and Mountaineer vehicles. All of the accidents were attributed to the original equipment Firestone tires, mostly the Wilderness model. The tire treads peeled off, and separated from the steel belts, while the vehicles ran at highway speeds, and avoidance manaeuvers from these incidents resulted in rollovers of the vehicles. Failing to persuade Firestone that it needed to replace those tires, Ford went ahead and replaced them for free, on its own, in the Gulf Coast countries, as well as Venezuela, Colombia, Ecuador, Malaysia and Thailand. Internal memos revealed that lawyers for Firestone and Ford had discussed the issue of having Firestone replace the tires, but Firestone's management was concerned that the U.S. government might see Firestone's replacements as an "admission" of safety defects, triggering an investigation, and an order for a U.S. recall. Neither company reported the problems they were having with the tires in these other countries to the U.S. National Highway Traffic and Safety Administration (NHTSA). At the time, no law required them to do so.

They approached the problem as a "legal" one and the companies fell into what I call the "myopia trap." This happens when management circles their wagons, jumps on the defensive, and focuses more on the company's "legal" obligations than on its responsibility to its loyal customers to "do the right thing," to assure their safety.

To be sure, Ford quickly recognized this, after Firestone announced its recall at a later date, and refused to widen the

number of tire models subject to the recall. Ford took the lead
and assumed responsibility to all owners of Ford vehicles by re-
imbursing them for the cost of replacing not only the tires in
Firestone's recall (which were limited to serial numbers from a
particular factory), but all of the Firestone tires of the same model
names, regardless of which plant produced them. Its actions cost
the company more than three billion dollars, and had a dramatic
impact in restoring goodwill with Ford's customers. This was a
giant leap out of the myopia trap, embracing the challenge of
"doing the right thing" for its consumers, despite the fact that it
significantly affected the financial health of the company.

Tapper's Tip #116

Looking at the short term in product liability issues, by putting
profits first, and deferring corrective action, while overlooking
the long term of maintaining customer loyalty, trust, and respect for your brand, creates a smoking gun that always comes
back to haunt.

So how did it all "hit the fan" in the U.S.?

An administrator at State Farm Insurance, a leading insurer
for automobile policies, e-mailed the NHTSA in mid-1998, to
advise of his concern about a disturbing trend of accidents involving 21 failures of specific Firestone tire models, 14 of which
were fitted on Ford Explorers. Despite this dangerous signal, the
agency took no action at that time. By spring of 1999, more accidents and deaths had mounted across the country. The NHTSA
finally began monitoring the tires more closely, and announced
the beginning of a full investigation in May, 2000.

The news media picked up on the story, and started following the evidence, piecing together the relationship between rollover accidents of Ford's Explorers and Mountaineers and certain models of Firestone tires. As the deaths related to tire tread separation kept increasing, the pressure mounted on Firestone to "do something."

Despite its earlier knowledge of problems with these same tires in other countries, and the increasing number of injuries and deaths in the U.S., Firestone's initial response was to deny anything wrong with its tires. Instead, it blamed the injuries and deaths on weather conditions, driver inexperience or error, or improper inflation pressure in the tires.

As the company pursued this hardline response, every form of news media was having a field day with front-page pictures and lead stories, reporting new highway deaths where Firestone tires were involved. In July, 2000, an issue of *Newsweek* featured a two-page color spread showing a father crying while kneeling beside his dead son, lying on the shoulder of a road. Alongside was an upside-down Ford SUV that had rolled over when a Firestone tire tread peeled off. Firestone's brand was clearly visible on the side of the tires. And this was just one story among others of parents mourning the loss of a child, or that of a promising college student paralyzed from the neck down—all of which resulted from similar accidents. The brand names of "Firestone," "Wilderness" (the tire model), and "Ford Explorer" were almost always mentioned in every news item, and in most cases, prominently displayed. The companies were suffering an unending, negative public relations bombardment, every hour, every day, and the coverage was worldwide for weeks. The media was closing in, arousing the public clamor to "do something," while the public's trust, and respect, for the brand were eroding dramatically.

Consumers with the reported Firestone tire models on their cars were restless, waiting in anticipation for the company to step to the plate to take care of their safety issues. The slowness to "own up" to responsibility to provide answers for Firestone's consumers, and take charge of the situation, forced independent retailers who were selling the tire brand to suspend sales, on their own, of the Firestone models involved.

Meanwhile, Ford, worried about sales of its hugely popular and profitable Ford Explorers and Mercury Mountaineers, and its continuing customer relationships, jumped in to salvage its own brands from the pummel of bad publicity. Ford's strategy was to disassociate from Firestone as a "partner." Ford's executives announced they were considering breaking the long-time contractual relationship with Bridgestone/Firestone Inc., as a supplier of original tires on its SUV lineup.

Eventually, Ford and Firestone broke their century-old association, and wound up publicly accusing each other's product as the cause of the deaths and injuries. Firestone, in a "misery loves company" maneuver, accused Ford of wrongly instructing its vehicle owners to inflate the Firestone tires with 26 pounds of air, instead of 30, thereby making the tires run "hotter" than they should, which allegedly increased the chances for a tread separation. Then it tried to blame Ford for making vehicles that were allegedly unstable in accident avoidance maneuvers, causing rollovers that contributed to more severe injuries. The public witnessed a finger-pointing match between two venerable companies that degenerated into an aggressive effort by Firestone to get U.S. Congressional investigative committees focused on Ford, and the stability of its SUVs.

Not surprisingly, lawsuit filings increased exponentially against both companies. They faced hundreds of them, which included scores of class actions. With accusations flying, Firestone and Ford each hired its own battery of engineers to study the real cause of the problems. The public questioned why, if they could get to the answers now, they didn't do so before over 200 people died in tire-related accidents.

Let's stop for a moment and freeze-frame the action. What

was happening correctly on Firestone's public relations level of crisis management? You guessed it: Nothing!

All of the right techniques, and effective rules, for handling the communication level of crisis management, had been ignored, or broken. The Firestone brand image took a nose dive and management appeared confused as to what to do next. The uncoordinated, undisciplined, slow, resistant, and inadequate responses seriously eroded the public's respect for the company's reputation, breached the public's trust, and disengaged their loyalty to what had been an immensely popular tire brand.

The brand's former popularity was crumbling, and there was no letup. The media relentlessly pursued stories that highlighted how Ford and Firestone had prior knowledge of the problems with the tires, and their connection to rollover accidents, and could have prevented many of the deaths and injuries had they taken some remedial action early on.

Finally, after waiting three weeks from the time the NHTSA announced its investigation, and having suffered the unforgiving daily barrage of negative news stories, Firestone succumbed to public pressure and announced a recall involving over 6.5 million tires. Company officials said they traced a manufacturing problem to tires made at its Decatur, IL, plant, so the recall was limited, mainly, to certain serial numbers attributed to production from that plant. Despite the enormity of the effort needed to replace 6.5 million tires nationwide, Firestone was simply not prepared to handle the crisis it had every reason to know would eventually come. The "myopia trap" came back to haunt it. The brewing pot had boiled over. It had no effective plan in place to handle the avalanche of consumers wanting immediate replacement of their tires. The vastness of the recall overwhelmed the company.

Ford stepped in to help by devoting some of its plants toward new tire production. More retail outlets were authorized to handle replacements for consumers who refused to allow replacement Firestone tires on their vehicles, and insisted on other tire brands which they felt were more "reliable." Other tire companies increased production, as Firestone eventually agreed to allow Firestone tire owners who had the model numbers of tires designated in the recall, to replace them with competitors' brands. An informal poll conducted by *USA Today*, reported that a month after the recall announcement, 39% of those surveyed said they would never buy a Firestone tire again!

In the meantime, while the public was demanding answers and Firestone was not supplying them, the U.S. Congress intervened and started hearings on "Who knew what, and when?" The top executives of Bridgestone/Firestone, Inc. agreed to appear before the hearing committee to answer questions under oath, in public. In an initial public relations blunder, Ford Chief Executive Jacques Nasser announced, through a spokesperson, that he was, in effect, unavailable to attend, as he was "busy" overseeing the production plant changes to meet the tire replacement demands. Talk radio hosts and TV pundits characterized the company as stonewalling, afraid to risk their Chief Executive having to reveal, under oath, for all the world to see and hear, how Ford "knew" of the tire problems for years, but failed to notify its SUV customers. Ford reversed its position in a few days when Nasser suddenly became "un-busy," and agreed to appear.

Finally, Ford's public relations department turned its focus to reinforcing the loyalty among its consumers, and their trust in the company's brands. Ford's financial picture took a beating from not only the tire recall, but additional recalls of its new 2002 model SUVs, as well as from hundreds of lawsuits that were settled involving the tire/rollover relationship.

The brewing pot—and the smell of smoking guns

The longer the crisis continued, the more opportunity there was for public disclosure of information acquired from independent investigations. Lawyers made progress through their pre-trial discovery in pending lawsuits, and revealed the internal documents they obtained through notices to produce. The news media quickly picked up on them keeping the drama "alive." U.S. Congressional investigators demanded turnover of more internal company memos, reports, and other documents, while news media reporters kept digging deeper for their own scoops.

When you have so many people handling documents, and so many are produced to different parties, in response to hundreds of lawsuits, and demands from regulatory agencies, the information in them is bound to leak. To understand why this crisis kept feeding upon itself, we need only to see how the public positions of the companies were contradicted by the internal evidence disclosed throughout the feeding season of the crisis.

Here's what the pot was brewing before it exploded:

1. Ford Motor Company first denied charges that it did not conduct a durability test of the Firestone tires on its Ford Explorer at the tire pressure of 26 pounds per square inch (which it recommended, as opposed to 30 that Firestone recommended) before the SUV went into production. It later reversed its denial, and acknowledged that such testing never happened on an actual Explorer, that the tests were on a test vehicle, which was a modified pickup truck, according to an Associated Press report [9/21/00 "Study Finds More Tire Trouble" by Nedra Pickler-Associated Press Writer, FindLaw Legal News]. *(It lost the credibility issue at the starting gate as soon as the gun went off.)*

2. Ford received "hundreds" of claims for defective tires between 1991 and 2000, according to warranty data, and among those were 148 claims for tread separation, according to a *Newsweek* report [September 18, 2000, 26-33]. *(Its knowledge caused the public to start associating Ford with the "do nothing" stance of Firestone, so Ford had to figure out how to break away from the*

growing negative image of Firestone.)

3. Congressional investigators uncovered three Firestone reports, from 1998, 1999, and 2000, showing "unusually high rates of failures and tread peeling from ATX II tires, one of the types involved in the recall." *(These were smoking guns of the first order rubbed in Firestone's face and displayed to the public whose opinion was growing into condemnation.)*

4. Firestone had contended that it first knew in July, 2000, that its Decatur, IL, plant was the primary source of the tires involved in the separations. But the reports showed that it knew, in 1999, that more than half the separation claims came from the Decatur plant. It appeared that the company had a similar report that included statistics for three years but company officials only analyzed the report for financial liability purposes without sharing it with the company's engineers for safety analysis. *(How do you think that information played in public while the company was trying to keep the public's trust? Here the pot was brewing and the company just kept it on the back burner. When it boiled over, can we really believe it was a "surprise"?)*

5. *USA Today* reported on September 6, 2000, that "Ford note from '99 reveals Firestone hid problem." The article discussed how an internal Ford memo from March, 1999, mentioned that Firestone didn't want to replace tires on Ford Explorers in Saudi Arabia because it didn't want to alert the U.S. government about the problems with the tires. The spokesperson for Firestone, however, had a different take on the memo: Firestone didn't replace the tires because there was no evidence of a tire design or manufacturing defect. As we mentioned earlier, the law did not require such reporting unless a manufacturer "knew of" a specific product defect relevant to U.S. consumers. *(Perhaps, consumers in Saudi Arabia use tires differently than their U.S. brethren?)*

The fallout

The mismanagement of the crisis had a significant impact on not only the tire industry, but automakers as well. Legislators focused on other companies who may have had knowledge of other tire problems. They quickly "beefed-up" existing laws to make sure companies would not repeat the behavior of Firestone. A new federal law made it a crime for company officials to withhold information about safety defects from government agencies. This forced automakers and their suppliers to report information to the NHTSA about warranties, claims, and accidents involving their products so it could address the issues more promptly and identify significant patterns that would signal alerts for consumers. The legislation also required the government to test vehicles for rollover potential, and imposed requirements on automakers to install systems that will warn vehicle owners when their tires are under-inflated.

These, of course, were positive effects for consumers. But, from an industry standpoint, Firestone and Ford's handling of the crisis forced more regulatory controls, and turned investigative agencies toward probes of other companies. Always watch the actions of other companies, and learn from their mistakes, as well as their expertise, because if you don't, how prepared will you be when the investigators start knocking on *your* doors?

Tapper's Tip #117

Whenever a company in your industry suffers a crisis, sound your wake-up alarms to look more closely at the pots on your own back burners, and make sure they're not brewing the same ingredients that caused the other company's pot to boil over.

The handling of the crisis had its internal toll, too, which was inevitable with such a devastating loss of brand value and market capitalization. In October, 2000, Bridgestone/Firestone, Inc. announced a management shake-up, reducing twenty-one divisions to four, with each reporting directly to a new chief executive officer. The intent was to improve internal communications to better coordinate trouble signals for product quality issues much faster.

Lawyers with suits pending against Bridgestone/Firestone announced to the media their concern that the company could not withstand the total damage claims they estimated as exceeding $50 billion, fearing the U.S. Firestone subsidiary may be forced to file bankruptcy. Bridgestone Corp., the parent company, quickly denounced the assertion and said it intended to set aside $450 million in 2000 to cover damage claims in lawsuits against the company. Nearly 180 cases were consolidated in a federal district court in Indianapolis. News reports noted signs of financial concern when the parent company announced that its sales of Firestone tires to consumers (as opposed to those it supplies directly to manufacturers as original equipment) fell 40% in September and October, 2000, as compared to the year earlier. Tire production at two plants was slashed and workforce reduced at Decatur, IL .

The Ford Motor Company, trying to repair the damage to its customers' experiences, announced that starting with its 2002 model Ford Explorers, buyers of its vehicles wouldn't have to rely on a tiremaker to take the lead for defective tire issues. Ford included "tires" in its own bumper-to-bumper vehicle warranty, bringing them under the Ford protective umbrella. It also moved quickly to settle lawsuits involving Ford Explorer rollovers set for trial so close to the introduction of its 2002 Explorer and Mountaineer models, which were touted as "redesigned," and "all-new," to spur renewed excitement in the brands.

Eight months after the recall announcement, Firestone engaged a multi-million dollar ad campaign, picturing its new President John Lampe, walking through a production plant. While doing so, he tells consumers that he's "in charge," that he made changes at the company with a new focus on quality control, that all this has come about "because your safety is our primary concern."

Will consumers buy that message after the wrenching ordeal the company put them through? At a National Manufacturer's Association conference in Nashville, Tennessee, in April, 2002, Lampe announced that he was "convinced" that his company emerged from the recall "stronger than ever," and Bridgestone/Firestone intended to make inroads with consumers by making and introducing new products.

Chapter 10

Lessons Learned: Managing PR

Avoiding "foot-in-mouth" blunders

The examples of Johnson & Johnson, Firestone, and Ford, provide valuable lessons for the best, and worst, way to handle a crisis. Without a formal public relations plan conceived, written, and practiced, BEFORE it all "hits the fan," your company is doomed to fumble its way through a crisis. If you don't learn from the mistakes of those who have "been there," you'll be doomed to repeat them.

That's why I'm giving you "Eight Rules You Need To Know for Crisis Management." Use these as your guide for setting up your PR operation to manage a crisis. They will alert you to the things you need to consider to customize your plan, according to your company's corporate "culture," the regulatory requirements of the industry or market sector in which it operates, and the uniqueness of its own internal operations. How, and when, you use them will depend substantially on the gravity of any crisis. Your goal should be to have an organized response system in place, ready to neutralize the negative effects of a crisis, whether it be a full-blown one, or a bad news incident.

Closely integrated with those rules are my "Eleven Commandments" for your spokesperson to follow in the grueling, unrelenting, and unforgiving world of the news media. These helpful directives will provide an anchor to stabilize, and fortify, your command of media relations, and temper the adverse effects when your company is in the bull's-eye of negative publicity.

The Eight Rules You Need To Know for Crisis Management-PR

➡ **Rule 1. Assemble and prepare your team NOW.**

A. Selecting the members

Carefully select the members that will become your Crisis Response Team (CRT). They should include the CEO, President, Sr. Vice President, and a VP of each major division, such as marketing, information technology, sales, production, and, of course, public relations, the General Counsel of your company, and the VPs of risk management and security operations. As soon as it's clear in a crisis which division has responsibility or involvement, the head of that division should join the CRT, if not already on it.

The number one person you must have for your public image during the crisis, the pivotal point person, strategically situated to convey the image your company must deliver is—YOUR SPOKESPERSON. Let me digress for a moment with a number of observations I've made, over the years, about spokespeople, regarding their selection, training, and demeanor. Although some of these points may seem self-evident, the blunders that companies make in their public relations make it clear they're ignored too often.

About Your Spokesperson:
Public Relations Tips

√ Select a person who is self-confident, articulate, at ease with public speaking, and exudes a warm, friendly appearance and demeanor.

√ Be aware of tone of speech, and ease of public speaking, when looking for the qualities this person needs. These traits need to convince the public of sincerity, concern, and understanding, which is quite different from the stiff formality of a bureaucrat reciting a lawyer-prepared "corporate" statement.

√ Although you should train several spokespeople for the position (as backups, if need be), make sure you designate, and empower, only one to be the official spokesperson at the time of crisis. The rest of the team must defer to that person for public comments. Otherwise, the smoke will rise when company officials offer contradictory statements.

√ This person must be capable of speaking your company's central message, without getting embroiled in a media sideshow reconciling the statements of other company officials that sound different than the core message.

√ Complete knowledge of your company's business is essential. Your spokesperson should be fully conversant about the operational procedures of all divisions of the company, including who the key operational managers are, and their functions, and the regulatory umbrella under which the company operates. Make sure you educate this person on the "issues," if any, the company has had with regulatory agencies, and the kinds of litigation in which the company is currently involved. Spokespeople must be brought up to date promptly on all of the facts that have anything to do with a crisis and its possible causes.

√ Be up-front. Many a story has been told about corporate people who get blind-sided by their own peers not telling them the "whole" story, before they face the press. Don't cultivate fertile grounds for smoking guns by allowing the spokesperson to assert false statements to the news media. An assertion that the company had no prior knowledge of any conditions alleged to be the cause of the crisis will surely backfire, at a later time, when plaintiffs' attorneys supply the media with documents that prove otherwise. Remember that in the pretrial discovery phase of litigation against your company, thousands of pages of documents will be uncovered, including reports, engineering analyses, and memos between engineers and senior executives. If the media gets hold of these, and their content clearly shows your spokesperson fed garbage to the press, you will have destroyed the company's, and the spokesperson's, credibility. It's all downhill from there.

√ An astute spokesperson cannot always rely on colleagues for "the whole truth and nothing but the truth." If you're the spokesperson, listen up: Be wary of what you hear as "truth," particularly, if you know otherwise. Ask lots of questions, and go to the right people for the answers. If you have suspicion that you're not getting a "confident" reply, or that you're not hearing the answer from an "authoritative" original source, seek out the original source and examine the evidence yourself. If you think you're getting the "run-around," or the officials who may have culpability for the crisis are stonewalling you, it's time to consider stepping down, instead of discrediting yourself, publicly, when your words backfire.

√ Adopt a one-voice policy. Your spokesperson IS "the voice." Advise employees that it's "company policy" to refer all news media questions to your designated spokesperson. It takes a corporate culture of honest and fair dealing with employees to make them feel a voluntary desire to see "their" company successfully sail through adversity. Many employees will be delighted to get out of the limelight in these situations, by knowing there is someone who is responsible in the company for handling outside news inquiries.

√ Employees need to know your communication policies. After making them aware of the company's spokesperson, and the responsibilities of that position, make sure that person becomes visible throughout the organization. Employees should readily identify the spokesperson's name, face, and office, for future reference.

Enough digression... now back to Rule 1.

B. TRAINING AND TESTING THE TEAM

Engage outside experts in the field of crisis management. They know how to train your team, and set up a crisis management profile that will outline the procedures to follow when faced with a crisis large enough to be a media event. The money spent now on this will be worth many times over its cost when you think how it could save your company's image and reputation.

Put the team to the test. Set up mock crisis situations. Provide a TV reporter simulation with video cameras, and have your spokesperson appear before the cameras to respond. Then, sit down, and have the team watch the videotape as if they were watching the evening news.

Provide critique and rehearse until it comes out right. Learn from your mistakes during drill time, not real crisis time. You can't afford to make mistakes in the midst of a real crisis because that may be a "bet the company" situation.

C. ESTABLISHING A CENTRAL COMMAND POST

Consider where you will set up a central command center. Here's where lines of communication are kept open for media, key management, and general employees. Organizational discipline is crucial in crisis response. You must show you're in control. There's no time for bumbling or fumbling.

Keep 24/7 contact. Know where the key members of the response team are located at all times. They should all be reachable at any time of the day or night, and their whereabouts (with phone numbers) should be updated daily. With cell phones, laptop computers, e-mails, and new wireless electronic gizmos coming on the market every day, there's simply no excuse for not knowing how to reach these important officials, 24 hours a day, 7 days a week.

Establish remote link-ups. Consider how to link your communications center with a remote center. Remember how the U.S. Presidential Election of 2000 focused for days and weeks on the state of Florida? The Democratic and Republican campaigns each moved people quickly, and set up operations in Florida where they could meet with the media, communicate with the public, and be right there, where all the action was taking place. Your company's plan should have a similar capacity.

Appoint a representative from each branch, or satellite location, to act as "crisis coordinator." In a time of crisis, this person will liaison with central communications at headquarters.

Consider creating a CRT at each of your company's loca-
tions. This is the better plan, because it keeps the people most
familiar with the local operations in charge of the communications. If you don't have that capability, have people ready to
travel to any location, and start reporting from the scene, so the
information will be firsthand, not filtered through numerous
representatives before the final version is delivered to the deci-
sion-maker in your organization. These people should become
thoroughly familiar with the physical facility and operation, at
each location, BEFORE any crisis develops.

➡️   **Rule 2. Know the difference between a crisis and a**
       story that's just bad publicity.

Don't over-react. Your response should be in proportion to
the extent of the crisis. Many times, a single story that reflects
negatively on the company, or its managers, requires little or no
response. The more you respond, the more you provide the in-
centive to keep the reporters reporting on a response-counter-
response basis. Most of these one-time stories fade from the
public's attention in a few days. On the other hand, if you're in a
real crisis situation, your response has to be at full-stage readiness. Certainly, if a tragedy occurs, with lives lost and injuries
mounting, there's no difficulty in identifying a real crisis at hand.

Identify the "in-between" stage. The difficulty comes when
the situation is in-between, where there may be personal injuries, but the connection to your product or your service is questionable, yet the publicity is negative. Your crisis management
team must make the decision on what kind of response is war-
ranted in these in-between situations. If negative publicity is
strong and persistent, it can quickly become a crisis for your
company's reputation. Get a quick survey of the public's perception, and prepare a response that addresses it.

➡ **Rule 3. Seize the day: The first 24 hours is yours**

No more "No comment." The media moves at the speed of light. When a story breaks, it's instantly all over the TV network news, with special reports interrupting regularly-scheduled programming. Quickly following are the Internet news media sites, the Web's chat rooms, bulletin boards, and all kinds of other Web sites. You can't afford to stay silent and unreachable to the media, or to send a mealy-mouse message of "no comment."

Your CRT is ON DUTY, front and center. Make information available to the media, and COMMUNICATE—openly, and honestly. As factual information comes in to the crisis command center from the scene of a disaster or tragedy, feed the facts to the media. Be open with them. Make them co-partners in getting the facts to the public.

➡ **Rule 4. Be truthful: Get in front of the issue!**

Be honest, forthright, and stick to the facts as known. This is no time for legal posturing and lawyer-worded statements that sound mechanical, vague, and self-preserving. (I'm not suggesting that you ignore your lawyers. Indeed, they're essential to this management process, not only for their legal expertise, but for their business acumen, but you shouldn't lose sight of the need to express a credible, and sensitive, message of concern.)

First things first. Your strategy will, of course, depend on the severity of the crisis. At the initial stage, your goal is to alleviate the pain of the crisis, and stabilize the forces that caused it.

Public's needs are first, the company's second. If done forthrightly and honestly, you should reap the reward of saving the company's reputation, and preserving the value of its brand. If you frame your initial responses to focus more on saving your company's hide, rather than taking care of the needs of victims and their families (if you're faced with a tragedy involving these elements), or addressing the fears and concerns of the public, you will lose the public relations battle, pure and simple.

Keep employees ahead of news coverage. Communicate with your company's employees in the quickest way possible, which is usually through the company's own network of e-mail. Make sure you are open and honest with employees about what they will hear in the news about the company, and what your management knows to be the facts, at that time, as well as what the company intends to do about it. Keep your employees well-informed, *ahead* of the general news media. If you know an adverse story is scheduled to be broadcast on local or network TV, or as a feature article in newsprint, alert them to it, and give them management's perspective of the issues. Remember, though, that some employees may forward your e-mail to their friends in other companies, so write as if you expect it will happen.

Cultivate employees as company ambassadors. Don't forget that your employees can be effective ambassadors in a time of crisis. Often, a neighbor of one of your employees will ask the employee to tell him what's "really" happening. If you keep your employees informed, and feeling "ahead" of the reported news, they'll be prepared to give the straight word. That neighbor then repeats it to other people, and the "word" spreads. You can nullify, or at least, assuage, the troublesome aspects of what your employees hear or see, news-wise. They'll acquire a critical view that observes whether the media is reporting fairly, as they know the facts to be.

Keep media up-to-date as you acquire new facts. The news reporters know when you're hiding something, and they can smell an insincere, canned speech recitation a mile away. Stay ahead of the issues by putting out information every few hours to show you are trying to be part of the solution to the problem, not a continuing factor in the problem itself.

➡ **Rule 5. Take charge. Act responsibly.**

Take Charge, Not Blame.   Don't equate "responsibility" with blame. Being responsible means you are taking the lead to help alleviate the immediate crisis, to help the victims, and provide humanitarian (and monetary, if need be) support for their families in the event of an ongoing tragic situation, such as violence in the workplace, or an explosion or fire. If it involves a product, and the public safety and health is in danger, it means you get in front of the situation and join forces with other authorities, such as regulatory agencies, to alleviate the immediate threats of continued danger.

Your cooperation is not an admission of wrongdoing. It's a catalyst to find the answers, and an aid in the investigation into the causes. You're in front of the problem, trying to solve it, wherever it leads. And the message you portray is your readiness to "do the right thing, whatever it takes."

Speak with sincerity. If your principal spokesperson speaks from only prepared statements that are not in comfortable speaking prose, and you portray a defensive posture, the public will think you have something to hide, or you're afraid to tell the truth. They'll know when you've put your own interest ahead of theirs.

Lawsuits are here to stay. Sure, you're worried about them. And let me assure you: No matter what you do or say, lawsuits will follow. You've heard the phrase, "Build it and they will come." Well, the same applies to lawsuits and crises, especially those involving allegedly defective products, or what appears to be injuries attributed to negligence. It's "Action News at 5, lawsuits at 7!" Plaintiffs are always out there. And as sure as a law of nature, predators will stalk a weakened prey.

Take a pro-active approach to thwart punitive damages. Consider this: By taking a "responsible" approach to stabilize the situation, you may set the stage to avoid punitive damages in future trials. The big money in jury verdicts comes from punitive damages. They're based on a jury's finding that your company's actions were callous and wanton, with an utter disregard—even maliciously so— for the safety, health, or well-being of your consumers. The more you step out in front, and make it clear with your words, backed by your company's actions, that your first priority is concern for the victims and their families, the more you take the wind from the sails of plaintiffs' lawyers who hope to paint a picture of your company as an evil villain deserving of punishment. So while it's probable your company will be a target for lawsuits, it can engage a strategy that will deny punitive damage entitlement to plaintiffs.

➡ **Rule 6. Use independent authorities to add credibility.**

Media reporting will usually slant in favor of consumers, and reflect the public's view of how Big Business cuts corners in favor of bigger profits. In every drama, there has to be a culprit, so reporters will keep digging to find the perpetrators of a crisis. The best way to defuse the fervor is to associate with reputable, independent authorities whose opinions are accepted as honest and fair. Here's what you can do:

Build a reputation for honesty and integrity. It helps tremendously with regulatory agencies that have oversight functions for your industry. The public tends to believe outside, and independent authorities, and the conclusions they make from an investigation. As preparation for crisis management, it's a wise strategy to stay in close touch, and on good, amicable terms with the regulatory authorities who oversee your industry's, and company's, operations. When your company runs a "clean" organization, in compliance with all rules and regulations, your officers get known for honesty and integrity, and that's bound to reap benefits when these agencies come to investigate the cause of a crisis.

Suppose your company is in the restaurant business, faced with a food poisoning outbreak. Local, state, or federal inspection authorities may inspect your premises to determine if the conditions are traceable to your company, or to your suppliers. If your company has had a stellar reputation with these authorities in "normal" times, the regulatory agents are less likely to fuel negative publicity on the crisis when they talk to the press. Diplomacy can go a long way in controlling how they report their findings.

Engage independent experts. If you're in situations where outside consultants have expertise in the subject matter, you could help your public relations by engaging these consultants to come in and determine the "facts" of how, and why, it happened, with opinions on how to correct deficiencies, if any.

Sometimes, the public's perception of your company will increase substantially by hiring a well-known person, respected for personal integrity and fairness, to lead an investigation into causes of the crisis. The public more readily puts aside its prejudice against big companies when a "neutral" person gets involved. It helps to remove the company's self-interest in the outcome, and provides credibility to the analysis, and findings.

➔ **Rule 7. Stabilize management: Preserve succession.**

Amidst the confusion of a crisis, your company needs stability in management. Your Chief Executive Officer and President (assuming they're two separate people) should not travel on the same airplane with the next two potential successors, or the next two senior executive officers. The Vice-President of the U.S. and the President never fly together on Air Force One. Follow their leads.

➔ **Rule 8. Stay tuned to the public.**

Survey your target audience. More than ever, your CRT needs some way of monitoring the public's feelings and reactions to your brand, and your company, during and after the crisis. You need to assess if you're on the right track in meeting the public's expectations. For your consumers who have been loyal to your product for years (and perhaps, generations), you'll want to know if they still have the "faith" in your product. Will they continue to buy your product in its "improved" version? Do they believe your company "did the right thing"? Or, was it too little, too late?

Monitor Internet sources. Don't neglect to check the Internet and the chat rooms, message boards, and newsgroups to find out what people are saying about your product and your company. Invest in third party professional monitoring companies that monitor the Web and notify you whenever your company's name or product is mentioned.

Keep your finger on the pulse of public opinion about your company. Focus your message to make it clear and effective.

The Spokesperson's Eleven Commandments for Media Relations

As with any response to the news media, crisis or not, there are precautions you should take. If you disregard them, you could be creating smoking guns. These cautions are rooted in principles that some professional politicians have mastered when talking to the media. That's why your spokesperson must be bright, articulate, knowledgeable about all operations of the company, knowledgeable about how the media works, and aware of legal consequences of stray statements. To avoid situations where your words come back to haunt you (as in future litigation against the company), your spokesperson, and any one else in your company who speaks publicly, should heed these Eleven Commandments:

FIRST: Stick to the facts. As information comes in, report only the facts, not speculation, not opinion, not hearsay. If you get a reporter's question that asks you to speculate, decline to answer, advising that, "I am not going to speculate, as that will confuse the matter. We're interested in reporting the facts as we know them."

SECOND: Don't give your opinion of conduct of others. Reporters may press for a sensational sound-bite from you, but you must resist. Bring them back to the facts, as you know them, at that moment. As more facts continue to develop, people can make their own judgment.

THIRD: Look out for the hypothetical questions of reporters. An example from a food contamination event: "What if the food poisoning were traced to your company's failure to follow hygienic procedures in packaging? What would your company say then, to the public?" Don't fall for these traps. They call for speculation, and remember, you're sticking to the facts right now.

FOURTH: Don't answer for someone else. Particularly, if it calls for your opinion as to what the other person would say in a hypothetical situation. Look out for the questions that start with "Suppose that...," or "What if...." If you're not giving opinions, you certainly don't want to speculate on opinions of other company officials. But, you can (and should) indicate a generic answer that higher officials in your company are extremely concerned, are monitoring the events closely, and want to do what is reasonable and necessary to prevent any further public harm, and bring stability to the events that caused the crisis—assuming, of course, that this is all true.

FIFTH: Don't get trapped by analogies and comparisons. Be careful of making analogies or comparisons of this event to things that happened in the past, or something that happened in another industry. Your comparisons may strike the wrong chord, may not be entirely accurate based on the emotions and facts in the present crisis, or in the one you use for comparison. As a result, plaintiffs' lawyers may turn these against you, later, to portray the company as having a shallow view of events, or callous disregard for the emotions of the victims and their families.

SIXTH: Stay "on" even if you're "off" the record. Don't get chummy with media representatives or let down your guard for "off the record" comments to them. Live by one credo alone: There's no such thing as "off the record," even if there is. You never know who overhears your conversation, or "misunderstands" that it's not for publication.

SEVENTH: Be aware of surreptitious tape recordings. Obviously, when you face the cameras and microphones, you know your comments are being broadcast. What you don't know is what happens at a lunch or dinner, when you may be meeting with a reporter and you think it's a private, casual conversation. Always be on guard and stay "on," if you're talking to anyone not in the company's close, inner management circle. If your conversation was recorded, you won't regret what you said.

EIGHTH: Learn the media rules of operation. Particularly, learn how giving "off the record" information for background purposes actually works. Many executives have been tripped up by giving information they thought was not for broadcast or publication, or not for attribution, only to find they didn't know the rules of the game, and the meaning of the terms used by media professionals.

NINTH: Don't give out any information unless it's accurate. Be sure it has been checked and double checked. Once you start a pattern of backtracking to correct previous misinformation you gave, your credibility with the public, and all media people, begins to erode. The name of the game in crisis management is credibility.

TENTH: When in doubt on how to phrase a controversial issue, consult with your company's lawyers. This is not contrary to what I've recommended before. We're talking here of terminology, not canned speeches containing formalized statements, written by lawyers. The news media may push you to admit, for example, that your company's foreman was "negligent," or that your company's product was "unreasonably dangerous" when it left your plant. These terms have legal consequences, and your wise counsel will advise you to avoid agreeing to them, as "admissions." To deflect such admissions, you may want to stick to a response that your company foreman "did not follow company procedures in place to avoid this event," instead of saying he was "negligent." An alternative response to admitting the product was "unreasonably dangerous" may be that the product "did not perform as expected." This comes down to "finesse" with words. A competent, skilled, professional spokesperson will know, not only how to spot these "live" grenades as they come at her, but how to throw them back, so they won't backfire. Your attorney is essential to this process. Educate yourself, and rehearse the kinds of "admission" questions that you could expect in the situations arising from the crisis, and be sure your attorney approves your responses. It's much easier, and safer, to deal with practice grenades than live ones.

ELEVENTH: Don't let the news media frame the issues. Use finesse to rephrase a question when, to answer it "as is," will box you into a difficult corner. If you want to observe professional spokespeople, and how to handle tough questions, watch the press conferences at the White House when the President's press spokesman spars with the news media. Notice one technique that's prevalent in responding to questions that are very touchy and controversial: the response is not to the actual question, but to one that the spokesperson rephrases, for a less controversial slant. By the time the spokesperson finishes responding, you've forgotten the original question, while the reporters have moved on. Some people call it finesse, while others refer to it as "the art of spinning." It comes with experience, and thorough preparedness. Before reaching the microphones, the spokesperson should anticipate all the tough questions that could be expected in a room filled with reporters who need sensational sound-bites and eye-grabbing headlines.

There you have it—the Eleven Commandments. They should serve you well, based on observations from the trenches. A highly skilled, articulate, and confident professional will make all the difference in the relationship with the media and the public—it'll either be "dancing with peers," or "dancing with wolves."

Your Spokesperson's
Eleven Commandments for Media Relations

1. Stick to the facts.
2. Don't give your opinion of conduct of others.
3. Look out for the hypothetical questions of reporters.
4. Don't answer for someone else.
5. Don't get trapped by analogies and comparisons.
6. Stay "on" even if you're "off the record."
7. Be aware of surreptitious tape recordings.
8. Learn the media rules of operation.
9. Don't give out any information unless it's accurate.
10. When in doubt on how to phrase a controversial issue, consult with your company's lawyers.
11. Don't let the news media frame the issues.

Eight Rules For Crisis Management-PR

Rule 1. Assemble and prepare your team NOW.
Rule 2. Know the difference between a crisis and a story that's just bad publicity.
Rule 3. Seize the day: The first 24 hours is yours.
Rule 4. Be truthful: Get in front of the issue.
Rule 5. Take charge. Act responsibly.
Rule 6. Use independent authorities to add credibility.
Rule 7. Stabilize management: Preserve succession.
Rule 8. Stay tuned to the public.

Chapter 11

Feeling the Pain

*Punitive damages and
the smoking gun connection*

Behind every big verdict—the kind in the high millions, sometimes, reaching into the billions—you're sure to find a punitive damage component that rocketed the damages into that atmosphere. Although these verdicts are usually the exception, rather than the rule, the public tends to perceive these as commonplace in product liability cases, just another Big Business getting its due.

The exception, you might say, was a case that captured everyone's attention, when a 79-year-old lady won a $2.9 million verdict against the fast-food giant McDonald's, after suffering third-degree burns from spilling coffee on herself at a drive-thru. Most people thought our civil justice system went awry, and were outraged that McDonald's had to pay such a large verdict that appeared to reward her for an action perceived as her own fault. (It never really paid that much, as we'll see.)

But did you ever hear what actually occurred in the courtroom during that trial? Did you know how smoking guns from testimony of McDonald's own officials, and information in its files, spurred the jury to punish McDonald's for its conduct? That story appears in this chapter, and there's much to learn from it to protect your own company.

Also here, is the story of how an old memo from a company engineer fueled a $4.9 billion (that's right, BILLION!) verdict in 1999, against General Motors, for a defectively-designed gas tank in a 1974 Malibu, that exploded in a rear-end collision, severely burning its occupants. The memo was a cost-benefit analysis that pitted dollars, and profits, against human lives.

Both of these suits involved product liability issues, but what else did they have in common? Smoking guns and punitive damages! And that's not surprising to those who have studied these cases. Smoking guns are common bedfellows with punitive damages. What a jury learns from a smoking gun inflames the passions of its members. They punish the wrongdoer by awarding the plaintiff huge dollars, so we call those damages "punitive." They're a special form of relief allowed when the plaintiff can prove the defendant's conduct was "malicious" and "willful." And they're in addition to what are known as actual, or "compensatory" damages.

Compensatory damages usually cover actual past, present, and anticipated medical expenses, physical therapy, lost wages, and what we all know as "pain and suffering." Although "pain" is an especially nebulous concept to describe, and even harder to quantify in dollar terms, it's firmly embedded in our damage award system in civil litigation. It's the area where the jury gets to reflect on how much it "feels" the plaintiff's pain.

Punitive damages, in contrast, do not "compensate" an injured plaintiff for pain, or any other losses. While they add substantially to the plaintiff's "take-home" award (and quite a

sum to the lawyer's fees), they're intended to punish the defendant. They're not granted in every case, but only in those where
the evidence warrants meting out such punishment. Many of
the states require "clear and convincing" proof that the
defendant's conduct was egregious enough to allow a jury to
consider imposing "punitives."

Before your company, as a defendant, can be hit with these
damages, the plaintiff has to prove your employees' actions, in
causing the plaintiff's injury, were beyond negligence, or a defective product design, or a defective product. They have to prove
an *intentional* disregard for the plaintiff's safety and welfare,
where the conduct can be said to be so offensive as to be "wanton," "willful," and "malicious,"— something way beyond their
neglect, inadvertence, or mistake.

To be sure, aside from the traditional purpose of punishing
the wrongdoer for such conduct, punitive damages are supposed
to have another special purpose: to send a warning signal to others who may be in the same industry, or similarly situated, to
deter them from engaging in the same conduct, or risk suffering
the same fate, or worse. The debate goes on as to whether they
actually have that effect, as by and large, companies don't "intentionally" set out to cause harm to their consumers. The
thing is, when we speak of "intentional" conduct as a required
ingredient for imposing punitive damages, the plaintiff doesn't
have to prove that you actually intended to cause harm. "Inten-
tion" is usually inferred when your actions are so unreasonable,
and dangerous, that a reasonable person (such as a juror) can
conclude that you either knew, or should have known, there was
a real likelihood that harm could result, and you consciously
chose to ignore those consequences. Your attitude of wanton-
ness, or abandonment of care or concern, is akin to "the devil be
damned." When that comes through clearly to a jury, be assured, they'll make the devil return, and you WILL be damned!

And what's better to show "intentional" conduct than a

smoking gun from your company's own files, or the testimony of one of your officers or other employees, revealing that management was aware of problems with the product, but either chose to do nothing about it, or tried to hide it? The most devastating kind of memo or report is the cost/benefit analysis where management analyzes what it would cost to correct an alleged defect in its product compared to what it would cost to make no changes but continue paying for estimated jury damages to consumers who are injured by the product. When a trial lawyer convinces a jury that the product, indeed, was defective in material or workmanship or design, and the jury sees the human cost vs. corporate profit analysis, the punitive damage engine is revving and roaring. Such is the framework for the close association of smoking guns with punitive damages.

Although I selected product liability issues to illustrate the connection between the two, be assured that punitive damages are not limited to product liability cases. You'll find them wherever the plaintiff can prove the "intentional" component that justifies them. I've seen them in suits involving gross negligence or employment-related claims where companies are found guilty of sexual, racial, or age discrimination. They're also found in sexual harassment claims, and in suits alleging violation of civil rights, particularly against excessive force by police (as in the Rodney King episode, in Los Angeles, several years back). Very rarely do you find a lawsuit awarding punitive damages in cases involving contracts or commercial law issues, unless they're combined with claims for fraudulent conduct.

Punitive damage "caps"

If punitive damages are supposed to "punish," the theory is that they must be large enough for a defendant to "feel the pain," only this pain is not of the muscular-skeletal variety, but of the depleted pocketbook type. Juries are allowed to consider the net worth and financial standing of a defendant to determine what it will take to make a damage award painful. Depending on the size and value of the company, punitive damage awards can be staggering, and many believe they are far out of proportion to the gravity of the injury suffered.

Fortunately, from the defendants' view, some states have addressed the problem, and enacted laws to "cap" the amount of punitive damages a jury can impose. These "caps" can vary widely, from an amount no greater than the total of compensatory damages, to a maximum of two or three times that amount, or a variable formula fixing the dollar amount based on the dollar range of compensatory damages. The efforts to "cap" are part of a political battle between those in favor of tort reform (to limit the number, and types, of lawsuits that can be filed, and reduce the amount of potential damages) and those opposed (including trial lawyers), who think the system needs no fixing, and argue the threat of unlimited punitive damages, and their unpredictability, are deterrents that keep companies vigilant about safety issues.

Supporters of reform argue that the end result only puts more money into the plaintiffs' pockets as a windfall. It also puts more into the pockets of the plaintiff's trial lawyers, particularly when those lawyers work on a contingent fee arrangement where they collect a percentage of the final damage award. Contingent fee percentages in individual cases are usually in the 30 to 50 percent range. In class action suits they fall into the 15 to 30 percent range, since the amounts recovered are so much higher, to compensate a "class" of plaintiffs.

Tapper's Tip #118

When you consider some of the punitive damage awards of hundreds of millions of dollars and, in cases involving tobacco company defendants, in the billions, it's not difficult to realize why plaintiffs' trial lawyers are so voracious in their appetites to find the right evidence that will carry their burden of proof to nail a company for punitive damages.

The unpredictability of punitives

The danger of punitives is in their unpredictability. Once the plaintiff proves enough against your company to warrant entitlement to them, the law provides no fixed standards for the amount, leaving it to the discretion of a hopefully, unbiased jury. These damages are supposed to bear some reasonable relation to the amount of compensatory damages, but this is the one area where juries get carried away with numbers, ultimately requiring the trial judge, or an appellate court, to reduce the jury's award.

In the General Motors case I mentioned, for example, the court knocked $3.8 billion off the jury's punitive damage number, leaving a final verdict of $1.09 billion against GM—by any standards, still a hefty amount for a single case.

Tapper's Tip #119

Although some of the huge jury awards you read or hear about in the news are actually reduced by trial court judges, who find them "excessive," or "unwarranted," or by appellate courts that review the case on appeal, that's not cause to ignore the potential of a verdict for punitive damages. As unpredictable as a jury's punitive damage determination is, so is an appellate court's review, or a judge's penchant for undoing the jury's decision.

The smoking gun connection to punitives

After having come this far in our journey through the world of smoking guns and paper trails, you should know what kind of evidence would make a plaintiff's trial lawyer salivate as proof your company had such a "conscious disregard of safety" that its actions, through officers and other employees, were "malicious, wanton, and willful." It could be a memo from one manager to another, or from a supervisor to the chief executive, that reveals your company's awareness of (but indifference to) safety and health problems involving use of your product. Maybe it's a file containing hundreds of complaints and personal injury claims that were resolved, quietly, because management chose to save the cost of a product recall, and take its chances that it would be cheaper to pay for injury claims as they occurred. Or, it could be tape recordings of executives' conversations, filled with racially derogatory remarks, in a suit by minority employees alleging racial discrimination. Perhaps it's the testimony of disgruntled front-line employees who, in a case involving violence in the workplace, speak of the callousness of upper management for ignoring their pleas for better security, and tighter screening of job candidates.

The trial lawyers' road to punitives is driven by a search for *knowledge*: whether management knew about a product and its connection to personal injuries, the extent of that knowledge, how it was acquired, and what steps were taken, if any, to deal with that information. Your company's files usually reveal all the evidence they need—the memos, reports, analyses, e-mails, tapes, and research papers. What your employees say in them, and how management reacts to them, are the keys to reaching the land of "punitive gold."

Tapper's Tip #120

The evidence for punitive damages usually comes directly from the companies that are trying to defend themselves against them. The courtroom showdown becomes the hangman's gallows, and the managers provide their own nooses! It's incredible, yet so true.

Let's take a look at real-life examples of how smoking guns and punitive damages are "naturals" together. Pay attention to the evidence the jury heard, and consider how it would have moved you, if you were sitting as an unbiased juror in the case.

The McDonald's coffee-burn case (Liebeck v. McDonald's Restaurants P.T.S., Inc.)

When the verdict from this case first headlined, many people were incredulous, convinced that our jury system had run amok. Conventional wisdom usually has the public siding with the individual who succeeds against Big Business, but from the way it was reported, the media, and the public, made a mockery of this elderly plaintiff. What they did not report may change your mindset on the case, so sit for a moment in the juror's chair, and consider your obligation to rule on the evidence. See how smoking guns can turn the tide of misconceptions.

The facts are, briefly:

> As a passenger in a car driven by her grandson, 79-year-old Stella Liebeck purchased a cup of coffee at the drive-thru window of a McDonald's restaurant in Albuquerque, New Mexico in 1994. Her grandson handed the cup of coffee to her, pulled over and parked, and Mrs. Liebeck attempted to take the lid off the cup.
>
> The car was an old model, with no cupholders, and the dashboard was sloped, so she held the cup between her legs and lifted up on the lid. The lid came up, but the coffee spilled onto her thighs, groin, and genital area, burning through sweatsuit material and all three layers of skin, before she could wipe it up. She sued McDonald's for gross negligence, and for strict liability, for selling and distributing an unreasonably dangerous product, namely, coffee, at an exceedingly hot temperature.

During the trial, the jury saw, and heard, the following evidence that moved them emotionally along the range from "frivolous," to "serious," to "deserve to be punished":

√ That it was officially known, through a public warning issued by The National Burn Center, that serving hot beverages with temperatures over 135 degrees Fahrenheit, risked severe burn potential.

√ That McDonald's served coffee at temperatures between 180 to 190 degrees Fahrenheit. (For comparison, testimony established that coffee at home is usually served at temperatures between 135-140 degrees.)

√ Through plaintiff's expert, testimony that a hot liquid at 180 degrees will burn through all three layers of human skin within two to seven seconds of contact, while reduced temperatures, at the recommended level, allowed significantly more leeway to wipe a spill, before a person would suffer any skin damage from a burn.

√ Through McDonald's own representatives, testimony admitting they *never* evaluated the safety aspects of the coffee temperature, despite the fact they knew the burn effects of liquids at that temperature. They acknowledged, without excuse, their focus was on maintaining optimum taste because it drove sales. McDonald's coffee sales revenues were approximately $1.35 million per day! They also admitted knowing that their coffee, as served (without waiting for cool-down), was too hot for human consumption.

√ The detailed description of the plaintiff's pain and suffering, including third-degree burns over six percent of her body, a hospital stay for eight days, and the several painful operations for skin grafting on her groin and genital areas. Her medical bills exceeded $10,000. Pictures of the burns presented gruesome, and graphic indications of the seriousness of the disfiguring injury.

√ **The first smoking gun:** From pretrial discovery, the plaintiff's lawyer discovered, from McDonald's *own* files, that McDonald's had handled over 700 burn claims due to its coffee temperature between 1982 and 1992, some of which involved third-degree burns very similar to the plaintiff's. They had settled most of these claims (which kept them out of the public records), and at least one of them was, reportedly, as much as $500,000. Yet, they still chose to make no changes to the coffee-serving temperature.

√ **The next smoking gun:** McDonald's own quality assurance manager testified that, despite the company's knowledge that a severe burn hazard existed at temperatures above 140 degrees, and despite the number of burn claims the company had been dealing with, the quality assurance staff's marching orders were to enforce the 180-190 degree standard, because "taste" was the singular focus, *not* safety.

With this evidence, as it played out in the drama of the courtroom, the plaintiff's case crossed the threshold of simple negligence, mistake, inadvertence or inattentiveness, to the justification for punitive damages: a showing of conscious disregard for the safety of patrons, in view of the company's knowledge of the hazards of its "taste-first" policy. The jury attributed 20% fault to the plaintiff for her own actions, and awarded her $200,000. in compensatory damages (reduced to $160,000. by subtracting her own 20% fault), along with $2.7 million in punitive damages, which amounted to approximately two days' revenue from McDonald's coffee sales. The trial court, later, reduced the punitive damages to $480,000., which is three times the compensatory amount.

We don't know the final number that was paid, because McDonald's and Mrs. Liebeck settled out of court, and reached a private, confidential agreement. (In the early stage of the claim, it was reported that McDonald's offered $800. to settle it, and initially, before retaining a lawyer, Mrs. Liebeck's family was seeking payment from McDonald's for only her medical expenses, which McDonald's refused to pay.) After the suit, a spot check by a local news reporter, in Albuquerque, found the coffee temperature at the local McDonald's reduced to 158 degrees.

The path to punitive damages was not hard to follow, and McDonald's supplied most of the evidence. Here's how McDonald's marched right into the verdict. Four actions that never should have happened:

1. Not correcting an injury-causing condition, based on 700 claims of injuries, from a coffee temperature that was too hot.

2. Setting quality assurance standards that emphasized "taste," over "safety," (where "taste" drove sales, and sales drove profits), instead of trying to find a compromise that satisfied both needs.

3. Under-estimating the emotional and shock value of graphic pictures of disfigurement and scars from third-degree burns, on a 79-year-old grandmother.

4. Not recognizing the impact of turning over files on 700 previous coffee burn claims, and the use to which a trial lawyer would put them, in the central theme of "profits first, safety second," and "Big Business vs. little old lady."

Now, let's look at somewhat different circumstances that foreshadowed punitive damages for General Motors.

The GM verdict *(Anderson v. General Motors)*

The facts are, briefly:

> An unemployed mother's four children, and an adult lady friend, on their way home from a midnight mass on ChristmasDay, in 1993, were severely burned when their 1974 Chevrolet Malibu's fuel tank exploded after their car was rear-ended at a stop light by a drunk driver, who failed to stop while speeding at 70 mph. The case was tried in Los Angeles, California, in 1999, where a jury awarded $107 million in compensatory damages—and $4.8 BILLION in punitive damages, against General Motors!

Beyond the actual damages, what could have prompted the emotional anger of a jury that imposed such a punishing verdict? The first thing you should be asking by now is, "Where was the smoking gun?"

This time, it was an internal GM memo, dated June 29, 1973, twenty-six years before the trial, but less than a year before the plaintiff's car model came out. Written by Edward C. Ivey, a company engineer in the Advance Design Unit, the now infamous memo is titled, "Value Analysis of Auto Fuel-Fed Fire-Related Fatalities," which is a cost/benefit analysis. He compared the cost of moving the gas tank location from just behind the rear axle to in front of it, to avoid fuel tank explosions from rear-end collisions, against the cost of death and injury claims from continued explosions, if GM were to do nothing. To make his cost comparisons, he estimated that each human life "has a value of $200,000."

Playing into the strategy of the plaintiffs' case, the memo

reinforced the central trial theme: profits over safety. Although General Motors denied that the placement of the fuel tank had anything to do with cost savings, neither the court, nor the jury, bought that defense. The Ivey memo had amortized the projected costs and estimated that deaths "where the bodies were burnt" were costing the company $2.40 per vehicle, based on the number of vehicles on the road with that fuel tank design, and the expected number, and cost, of fatalities. He concluded, it would be "cost effective" if the company were able to relocate the tank, and spend no more than $2.20 per new vehicle to change the design and "prevent a fuel fed fire in all accidents."

The memo ends with a feeble attempt to temper the callousness of the earlier remarks. Here's the last paragraph with my editorial comments interjected:

> "This analysis must be tempered with two thoughts. First, it is really impossible to put a value on human life. [ed. note: *But he did it anyway!*] This analysis tried to do so in an objective manner but a human frailty is really beyond value subjectively. [ed. note: *I guess that means the company can't make a decision unless it's based on dollars so, to make it work, he had to equate humans with a dollar value.*] Secondly, it is impossible to design an automobile where fuel fed fires can be prevented in all accidents unless the automobile has a non-flammable fuel."

The tone is out of character with the callous calculations that preceded it, almost as if the paragraph were inserted for protection against a future reading that the author knew would inflame the sensitivity of ordinary people. This kind of protective language didn't serve its purpose because it was disingenuous, out of sync with the main theme of the memo. It only emphasized insincerity, and above all, missed the point: No one was asking that GM design an automobile "where fuel fed fires can be prevented in all accidents." The question the plaintiff's lawyer hammered away at was why GM didn't commit the $2.20 per vehicle to move the fuel tank and improve the chance that these four children, and one adult, would have been spared their disfiguring burns.

Throughout the trial, GM's defense was bombarded with a supply of internal documents, originally collected by other trial lawyers, who shared them from their nationwide collection bank involving other cases with fuel tank fires in GM's cars. It was reported that as early as 1971, documents showed that GM's engineers were required to justify, with a cost-benefit analysis, any safety improvement they recommended that exceeded the National Highway Traffic Safety Administration's minimum requirements. Documents like these simply fed a trial lawyer's favorite, central theme of "profit before safety," over and over again, and the jurors heard it loud and clear.

How much is "enough" to "feel the pain"?

Jurors have no mathematical formula (other than the "caps" of state law, if they are in a state that has them) to determine amounts to award. The wealthier the defendant, so it goes, the more it will take to make him "feel the pain." In a majority of states, if your company were the defendant, the jury would consider evidence, such as:

- your company's annual income
- your company's annual gross sales revenue
- how much your company spends on advertising (presumably, if it can afford big dollars on advertising, it can afford to pay punitive damages)
- profits before, and after, taxes
- the value of your company's receivable and payable accounts

- the annual income taxes your company pays
- the overall value of the company's assets, including buildings, land, furniture, fixtures, equipment and "goodwill"

In the *Anderson v. General Motors* case, the plaintiff's lawyer used the Annual Report of General Motors for 1998, and read to the jury the numbers from the financial section, citing average annual sales of $162 billion, an annual advertising budget of $3.7 billion, cash on hand of $10.8 billion, and so on. An interesting, and detailed, article in *The Wall Street Journal* (September 29, 1999, by Milo Geyelin) described the drama of the trial, and quoted Pedro Martinez, one of the jurors who was interviewed after the verdict was announced. Martinez summed it up succinctly:

> "We saw the figures, the amount of money that General Motors was spending on advertising and also how much money in sales every year...We thought that General Motors had to be punished somehow. **We wanted to send a message and not just to General Motors but every manufacturer...when they know something is wrong and they don't want to fix it.**"

There you have it. The plain and simple truth in the world of consumers (who, by the way, are also jurors) and how they perceive Big Business when consumer welfare and profits are in the balance.

Product Liability and Punitive Damages: Reducing Your Risks

Many of the gargantuan damage awards you hear about are from the product liability world. The kinship between punitive damages and product liability is all too evident. And the way to protect your company from such adverse verdicts is even more so.

When jurors are questioned after deciding verdicts in civil cases, they consistently mention the issue of safety vs. profits as foremost in their minds when deciding liability. They ask whether the company was concerned with the safety of its consumers. Did it put profits first, ignoring the danger signs of problems with its product, and the potential risks faced by its consumers? Did the evidence point to an attitude showing the consumer's welfare as secondary, with the company's bottom line profits as primary?

Tapper's Tip #121

As simplistic as it may seem, in the product liability arena the single, most effective way to avoid the kind of evidence that backfires, is to adopt a corporate mission of "Safety First!"

That doesn't mean just lip service, but a matter of leadership and commitment. Management must consistently demonstrate in communications to employees, and in the quality assurance standards, that nothing comes ahead of "safety" as the first priority for the company's mission to consumers, and employees should be evaluated on how they contribute to this mission.

The simple fact is this: If your company intends to protect itself against punitive damages in the product liability area, it must face reality from a consumer's side. The consumer's perception *is* reality, and it's difficult or impossible to change that. And remember that jurors are selected from a population of consumers. If your company can't show its dedication to consumer safety, in words and actions, by the time of its next product liability suit, get prepared for a precipitous plunge into the punitive damage pool.

If you're serious about considering how to support a "Safety First" commitment, from a litigation perspective, to reduce the risk of punitive damages, then consider this advice:

1. No more cost/benefit human life comparisons. Forbid all cost/benefit analyses that compare the price of sacrificing human lives against the costs of improving faulty designs, or correcting defects in products. I'm not suggesting the end of all cost/benefit projections, just those that use human lives as a factor for sacrifice in the projections of costs.

Tapper's Tip #122

If you de-value the sanctity of human life by calculating the cost of sacrificing a life, against the cost of improving or repairing a known problem with your product that could injure or kill people, you should expect your company to sink into the quicksand of punitive damages. It's only a matter of time.

These reports or memos, all of which are discoverable under pre-trial discovery rules, could one day be your roll of the dice in a "bet the company" lawsuit. Do you want to be the supervisor who requested the memo? Or the President, or CEO?

2. Thoroughly investigate, with objectivity, all issues that signal defects. Adopt internal procedures that centralize communications about product problems, whether they be issues of design, process, sales, distribution, or advertising. Establish a committee to read and review each and every claim or complaint about the product, and put members on the com-

mittee from each department or division, including engineering, marketing, finance, general operations, physical facilities,
risk management, and security. Be aware of territorial jeal-
ousy, where a department member doesn't take the objective
position in dealing with an issue over a possible design defect.
Department people that react defensively, rather than objectively, to a complaint, can be trouble for your company. What
you don't need are people who rationalize the virtue of their
own position, or those who deflect criticism by denigrating the
critic. More than one complaint on the same issue should signal the need for greater focus and attention.

3. Be prepared for recall. Issue a general recall when
you have enough evidence that the problem is a design issue, or
manufacturing defect, that could affect a consumer's safety. The
best timing for a recall is when there have been no reported injuries, and you have evidence of a "defect." A prompt recall nips
the issue at its core, and can effectively undermine any of the
class action hunters that are always out there. If you blow the
timing issue, and only recall a product after many injuries, and
only when forced to do so by public opinion or regulatory edicts,
you're not only putting your own career on the line (for poor
leadership and foresight), you're also risking the value of your
product's identity by brand, and perhaps, the reputation of your
company.

4. Tighten and enforce quality controls. Initiate
tighter quality assurance controls throughout the manufacturing process to assure that problems don't escape the production line. Is there a procedure in place to deal with below
standard specimens? Does your workforce feel that you address quality control issues promptly, and with integrity? Or do
they have the impression that supervisors and managers get
lax to meet quotas for their own survival? Is there a cynical

attitude among the employees, or an honest, good feeling about the dedication of management to producing a quality product, whatever the cost?

How do you test this attitude? Hopefully, not by having managers and supervisors ask their own subordinates. Not if you want honest answers. I'm referring to open and free expression, without fear of retribution. You can accomplish that, most effectively, with an outside consultant that performs periodic reviews. Barring that, your human resource department might design a survey instrument that provides for anonymity in the response, to ferret out issues among employees.

5. Listen to your workforce. Complaints from them should be handled in the same manner as if they were coming from your consumers. Investigate, and follow-up, each issue. A stressed, and overworked, production crew will create problems somewhere along the line, and problems become defects at the end of the line. A workforce that thinks highly of the company it works for, and feels proud of the company's culture, produces far better quality products than a disgruntled, antagonistic crew. Listen to your front-line. They often provide valuable insight that should not be overlooked.

6. Build and maintain a happy work force. Don't underestimate the power of employee morale as an important tool in avoiding smoking guns. Having happy employees who feel good about their company and its management goes a long way in your favor. When they're called upon to provide deposition testimony about daily operations, how problems are handled, and how responsive the management is to issues, you'll reap the benefits many times over from their upbeat attitude. It will directly affect the quality, and usefulness, of their testimony for the company's defense. Contented people are eager to express the pride in their work, and the appreciation they receive from their supervisors. When the plaintiff's lawyer tries to coax them into expressing negative opinions about their job, and the way managers handle their concerns, they will be ready to dispel the lawyer of such notions.

7. Educate your management to the other smoking gun traps. Don't forget the other traps that get businesses in trouble—the ones that are discussed throughout this book. Your management should attend training workshops to stay alert to the traps that trigger smoking guns, and reinforce the skills and techniques to avoid them.

Wisely, every manager and supervisory employee should have a copy of this book for reference and a daily reminder. If you find their copy isn't showing signs of wear and tear after six weeks, lower their performance evaluations! (Just a suggestion; it sounds good to me.)

Chapter 12

Act Now or Pay Later!

Document retention...and more

We've seen how the opportunities to create smoking guns pervade the workplace, and everywhere else you conduct business, from desktops to laptops to palmtops, desk phones to cell phones, and from home to the main office. It's time to ask yourself some basic, but important questions.

How does your company gain control of the volcanic mountain of information before it erupts, and buries all?

How can you reduce the potential for liability when employees misuse the e-mail system and the Internet during work hours, and accumulate paper documents in desk drawers, file cabinets, and storage boxes?

What can the company do about computer-based documents that employees keep producing like a ticker tape on a busy stock exchange? They proliferate with wide, unchecked distribution, and get backed up on the company's servers, indiscriminately, regardless of any need to keep them.

If you want to get a grip on this, you need to seize the initiative by drafting, and implementing, policies on document retention, and e-mail and Internet use. You must also train your employees on their meaning, purpose, and enforcement. If you act now, you can avoid suffering huge losses in future litigation, by reducing the incidence of smoking guns, and eliminating the files you no longer need that could be housing them.

But don't think that simply drafting, and labeling, a policy is enough. How effective your policy will be depends, essentially, on your top management's commitment to making it work! Once in place, a policy succeeds only if you integrate it into your corporate culture, keep employees aware of it, and make sure all terms are clear, and easily understood. And most of all: Apply, and enforce, the terms of each policy consistently, and across the board for ALL employees, at every level. Enforcement cannot be sporadic. If your company is lax in applying or enforcing these policies, they'll backfire somewhere down the line. It might be from an employee who claims they were applied selectively, and in a discriminatory manner. Or, it may be when an opposing attorney accuses your company of using the document retention program as a subterfuge for selecting, and discarding, "bad" documents, at the company's convenience. So, don't deceive yourself into a false sense of security if your policies are merely window dressing.

These policies do work well, when drafted properly, and enforced consistently. They're not a panacea for avoidance of all liability. Neither are they a substitute for instructing and training your employees on good writing habits, and how to avoid the pitfalls and traps we've covered in the previous chapters. When effectively implemented and enforced, however, these policies, in conjunction with peristent instructional training of employees, are a strong element in your arsenal of controls to reduce, or eliminate, the safe harbors for smoking guns.

I'll provide you with essential points that should be covered when drafting and implementing them. Each policy should be tailored, though, to the unique needs of your company, and reviewed by your attorney to be sure it meets all applicable state and federal laws, and the rules and regulations of regulatory agencies that govern your company's business, and the industry in which it operates.

What is "document retention"?

It's a process, described in a written policy, where you identify the documents you have, and how long they should be "retained," and when they should be disposed of, including the manner of disposal. When we speak of "documents," the term includes the whole panoply of information, from paper correspondence, memos, contracts, blueprints, designs, and artwork, to computer-based data, such as spreadsheets, word-processed files, and e-mails. Some companies refer to their policy as a "Corporate Records Management Program," or a "Document Retention and Disposal Policy."

Whatever you call it, the object is to clean out documents that you no longer need to keep. Not on a "pick and choose, when convenient" basis, but according to a systematic, organized, and categorized business plan that controls document storage, which is part of your company's regular operations. The benefits come from freeing up storage space, ridding the company of unneeded information, reducing the costs of maintaining storage, and significantly reducing the potential of liability from old documents, no longer relevant to your current business, but always capable of misinterpretation in the wrong hands.

Spoliation of evidence? Sounds like a disease.

When it comes to document destruction (the flip side of document retention), there are some serious warnings and alerts you need to know about.

WATCH OUT for the DANGER ZONE! When you're on notice of a pending or threatened lawsuit or official investigation, you have an obligation to retain all evidence, of any kind, that may be relevant to it. If you breach that obligation, the courts (in state systems, as well as federal) may impose sanctions against you, particularly if it appears your actions were intentional. In civil litigation, destroying such evidence, or not taking reasonable measures to protect and save it, is referred to as "spoliation (for "spoiling") of evidence." This is a very serious violation, and every court system has specific rules of procedure to deal with it.

The severity of the sanctions rests in the discretion of the court, which can range from imposing fines and penalties on the offender (also called "the spoliator") and curtailing your right to raise certain defenses, to instructing the jury that it's allowed to conclude the reason your side didn't produce the evidence the plaintiff had requested was because it would have exposed damaging information against you. This sanction is referred to in the law as "adverse inference."

In still other cases, the court has even entered a "default" against the spoliator, the effect of which is to declare you liable to the plaintiff for whatever the plaintiff's pending claim is against you; no need for plaintiff to show any further proof. The only thing for the jury to decide, when that happens, is the amount of damages. It works both ways, though. If your company, as a defendant, has proof that the plaintiff has destroyed relevant evidence, the plaintiff's lawsuit may get dismissed, as a court-ordered sanction.

> ## Tapper's Tip #123
>
> Spoliation includes the failure to preserve evidence when you know, or should know, of its relevance to a pending, or threatened claim. Your opponent has a heavy burden of proof to convince the court of wrongdoing, in this regard, but once proven, your company is cast with a damaging negative image, not only with the jury, but with the public, who will read the newspaper headlines portraying your company as a rogue.

Both state and federal criminal statutes may also come into play. You can find them under such labels as "tampering with evidence," and "obstruction of justice." These refer to criminal offenses where evidence is destroyed, after having knowledge that an official proceeding or investigation is under way. They also include any attempts to conceal evidence, or hinder discovery, or the apprehension, prosecution, conviction, or punishment of a person for a crime. Assisting someone to commit these acts makes you just as guilty as the person actually doing them.

In the wake of the Enron Corp. bankruptcy in 2001, the world heard that its outside auditing firm, Arthur Andersen LLP, engaged in document shredding in their Houston, Texas office. Although shredding, in and of itself, is not usually a problem, it becomes a major one when it's done in the face of impending investigations into questionable accounting practices, as was the case with Enron involving off-the-books partnership deals. As a result of the shredding, the U.S. Justice Department filed an unprecedented criminal indictment against the Arthur Andersen LLP accounting firm for obstruction of justice. Andersen's senior auditor plead guilty to a criminal obstruction charge, and acknowledged his direct involvement in the illegal activity.

Spoliation is a matter of timing. You can't expect to discard documents, without repercussions, when you know of wrongdoing, or at least, questionable practices subject to regulatory investigations that are pending or imminent. And when you're in a publicly-owned corporation where officers have a fiduciary obligation to shareholders, the effects are compounded. Arthur Andersen's reputation as a Big Five accounting firm tanked over this debacle. As a defendant in hundreds of suits by Enron shareholders and employees for losses suffered by the precipitous plunge in Enron's stock value when it all "hit the fan," Andersen faced liability exposure to not just millions, but hundreds of millions of dollars.

Document Retention Policy: Guidelines and suggestions

Beyond the limited reach (and nasty connotations) of spoliation, however, companies have every right to clean out their documents periodically, as a business necessity. No one expects a corporation to forever archive all of the electronic files and paper documents it generates from day to day. Not only would that reach impossible proportions, particularly in large corporations with thousands of employees and hundreds of "branch" operations, but the cost of storage facilities would soon become prohibitive, as the space available for such storage gets more costly and difficult to manage.

For those companies with a huge backlog of paper and electronic files that have never been "cleaned out," the task will be daunting. But start you must, if you desire to avoid huge legal exposure in your future, and the costly expense of sifting through, sorting, and producing all of this information in the next lawsuit. The more you have inside your company, and in storage, the greater your burden to produce documents in litigation. For aggressive trial lawyers, the more you have, the more they'll demand. Some hard labor and sweat now will pay off many times over. If you do nothing, on the other hand, your volcanic mountain of paper and electronic files and messages will keep accumulating, rumbling louder and louder, until it erupts when you least expect it. Unfortunately, that's usually with the next class action lawsuit that comes your way.

While you're deciding if you want a document retention policy, use these guidelines and suggestions about how to approach it and make it work effectively:

1. Make sure senior management buys-in

You can't have an effective policy unless senior management buys in to the fact that information generated within the company, in whatever form, is either a strategic asset, or a potential liability. The effort should be headed by a top management team that studies the entire company, and its information work flow. If you have a law department, look there for a chairperson to head the team, and be sure to include your company's Chief Privacy Officer, if there is one. Otherwise, appoint an executive member who has demonstrated organizational and management skills, and who has been with the company for a significant length of time. Include members from each major department, or division, on the team. Knowing the company, its operations, and the work flow process, puts your team ahead at the start.

2. Take document inventory from top to bottom

A document retention plan requires detailed identification, and categorization, of documents your company has in its midst. You have more than you think. To give you some idea, here are some of the categories:

letters, memos, printouts from computer files, general

corporate records (annual reports, proxies, financing statements), legal files and papers, contracts, pension documents, union documents, insurance records, risk management files (including claims), accounting and finance records, payroll records, personnel files, tax records (including tax returns, schedules, supporting information), safety and environmental records, research and development documents (including lab test reports, product tooling and design specifications, and research data), quality control and inspection records, sales and marketing materials, customer records (including credit information, financing agreements, consumer credit applications), and "general" (books, periodicals, trade magazines, outdated corporate, and division policy and procedure manuals)

3. Assign realistic retention periods

For each category of documents, establish a holding period, or "retention" date. For example, you might decide that invoices for supplies may be retained for a maximum of two years, in which case, all invoices over two years old should be discarded. Your counsel, however, will need to consider warranty periods because your purchase invoice can provide date-of-purchase proof, should you need to invoke a warranty. Drafts of contracts may have a retention period that expires upon execution of the final version of the contract. Once the contract is signed, you may decide to discard all prior drafts. The time schedule will vary, depending on the category of document, and the specific kind of document in that category. Some documents will require "permanent" retention, such as incorporation records, licenses, deeds, bills of sale, etc.

The most perplexing part of assembling a document retention program is deciding which retention dates are appropriate for each item. This aspect of preparing the document retention policy should be reserved for your company's attorneys, exclusively. Using the wrong dates, and destroying a document too early, for example, could cause difficulties with regulatory agencies that require specific records to be retained for a designated time. Your company's attorneys have significant considerations to take into account: state, and federal record-keeping requirements based on your industry, and the business your company transacts, regulatory requirements, statutes of limitations for personal injury claims, contract claims, employee lawsuits, Internal Revenue Service record-keeping requirements, union contractual terms, and others.

4. Make compliance mandatory

Once the categories, items, and retention dates are established, the program must require the purging of files as a mandatory undertaking. If you allow the selective "picking and choosing" by each employee of whether to "save" or "destroy" a document, the program may backfire on your company. Courts recognize a formal, written document retention program that provides for aged document destruction, with reasonable holding periods, for good faith business reasons. When your program becomes "selective," however, it starts taking on the appearance of a bounty hunt for "bad" documents. Then, if you can't produce a document the other side knows you should have had, the inference will be that you destroyed it because you knew of its harmful effect. The next word you'll hear with that inference is "spoliation." If you can show it was destroyed, without "special" selection, and as part of the general program outlined in your policy, you should be able to convince a court of your company's good faith.

5. Search for, and destroy copies

Because documents are stored in so many ways, and copies are made and distributed to too many people, your team has to tackle how to round up all these copies that are earmarked for destruction. When you find a paper document in a file, it may have the persons listed on it who were sent copies, so their files will also need to be checked. It makes no sense to clean out aged originals of documents, only to find later, in a pre-trial discovery, that copies of these documents turn up in the archived files of management associates.

Determine if the creator of the document may have it stored on a computer's hard drive, floppy disk, or other storage medium. Don't forget off-site computers for any employees who work at home. Laptops should be checked for their contents, too.

6. Don't neglect informal, everyday documents

Document retention programs usually refer to formal company documents. But don't lose sight of the volumes of "informal" documents that employees generate everyday: drafts of memos, letters, contracts, and proposals; calendar diaries that have revealing entries and personal notations; handwritten notes; telephone logs that show every phone call, made or received; and correspondence logs that chronicle every written message sent by that employee to anyone in, or out of, the company. These items should be purged as soon as their usefulness has passed. Executives rarely need their calendar/planners from a few years ago, or their personal trip reimbursement reports from several years past.

7. Decide where computer-based documents belong

Decide if computer-based documents, including e-mails, are to be part of your general Document Retention Policy, or included in a separate Electronic Document Retention Policy. The files in electronic storage, including back-up tapes from the company's servers, are especially important to purge on a systematic basis. The amount of information stored on CD-ROMs or back-up tapes that fill one file cabinet drawer could be the equivalent of a warehouse full of documents in archival boxes.

It's all too easy to overlook the mass of aged information, and potentially harmful files (when you consider the breeding grounds that e-mail provides) in electronic storage. Assign specific procedures and policies to target electronic information.

8. Take account of holding periods required by law

All records needed for substantial compliance with relevant laws and regulations, applicable to your company's business and industry, must be identified, maintained, and safeguarded for at least the minimum periods required by any such laws.

In those instances where records have a retention period mandated by law, precautionary measures should be implemented to be sure those records do not get destroyed prior to the expiration of that date. Otherwise, you will raise suspicion of bad faith, and may incur penalties within the law or regulation that mandated their retention.

9. Protect vital records

Identify, protect and safeguard vital records. These include your company's original charter, by-laws, registrations, licenses, patents, real estate deeds, certificates of title to fixtures and equipment, and things of that nature.

10. Avoid spoliation claims

Fail-safe provisions must provide a sure-fire way to halt destruction of records when you or your colleagues acquire knowledge of a new lawsuit filed against the company, or there's a threatened lawsuit, a governmental inquiry, or an investigative project where your company is sharing information with outside agencies. Your company's attorney must then examine the issues involved, and determine what part of the retention program can go forward safely, without running afoul of spoliation issues.

11. Consider hiring an outside records management company

An outside records management company can handle not only the safe-keeping of your stored records, but the proper disposal of those records scheduled for destruction. These companies have massive paper-shredding machinery that will do the job right.

Tapper's Tip #124

If you dispose of records on your own, beware of the pitfalls of improper disposal; avoid creating another problem by careless handling..

Don't get lax by not following the trash trail to the shredder. Check the background of the shredding company, and ask to see the files of the employees who are in charge of the shredding. Do your own background check with the information you obtain. Be sure adequate security procedures are in place in any such company before you make any commitments. Get them to sign a confidentiality agreement to protect against disclosure of any documents that might be readable during the shredding process. And consider stationing your own employee at the shredding site to oversee the operation.

12. Apply policy consistently across-the-board

Consistency is important. Apply your records management to the whole company, not just to some departments, while you grant exemptions to others. If e-mails are to be purged every six months, then every department and every employee from CEO down must comply.

Tapper's Tip #125

If an opposing counsel can point to "selectivity" or inconsistency in your document retention program, it's another opportunity to raise suspicion and accusations of bad faith against your company.

13. Anchor your policy with a good-faith business purpose

Courts will look for a formal, written policy, with reasonable retention periods that show a bona-fide business purpose. They'll also check for evidence of enforcement on a consistent, non-selective basis. When an opposing counsel complains about your company not producing a document that counsel thinks you should have had in your files, a court will be more inclined to consider the document was destroyed, in good faith, if you have a legitimately-based, and consistently enforced, policy.

14. Position your policy as a strategic risk management function

Records management is a strategic function, and should be considered a risk management priority. Companies with adverse jury verdicts for millions of dollars are almost always victims of their own documents, generated, collected, and stored inside the company. As such, records management should be viewed as a compliance policy, subject to the internal audit process, just the same as other compliance issues like insider trading, conflicts of interest, and receipt of gifts from outsiders. The audit will assess the effectiveness of the records destruction process for its consistent and systematic application. It can also assess the records inventory to verify that records that should have been discarded were, indeed, destroyed in accordance with the Document Retention Policy guidelines.

15. Adopt clear enforcement guidelines

Be specific on the enforcement procedures, and assign responsibility for their administration to one department. Human resources, or the law department is usually best equipped to take over this function. Let employees know, ahead of time, the consequences of non-compliance.

16. Educate employees

Your policy will work only when employees perceive top management's commitment to its letter and spirit. Training is essential, and it should start at the orientation of new employees, and continue with periodic reinforcements. Make sure the training emphasizes the good faith business purpose and benefits of the policy. Keep the emphasis on reduction of information overload, and deflate sinister notions, or rumors, that it's a "get rid of bad documents" exercise. When you follow the policy, and require destruction of documents simply because the time is up for their retention, this goes a long way in controlling any snide undercurrent.

E-Mail and Internet Use Policies

Effective E-mail and Internet use policies require clear definitions of what is acceptable, and unacceptable, use of the company's e-mail system, and Internet access. For the company's benefit, it's real important that you provide a method for daily acknowledgment by employees who use the system, of their awareness of the policies. The terms should be available for viewing at all times as a computer-based file, through a link on the company's internal network.

Tapper's Tip #126

To reduce the chance that an employee will later complain that he "wasn't aware" of the policy, access to the e-mail program on the company's local network should be barred, until the employee has to answer, by clicking a button for "yes," or "no," on an initial screen that asks if he understands the e-mail usage policy (include the Internet policy if you have one), and agrees to abide by its terms. A "yes" click allows the program to open, while a "no" click denies him access, and takes him to the pages where the policy is posted. The "no" should also deny access to any Web browser that would enable access to the Internet.

Most of the litigation filed by employees against companies involving e-mail use has centered on charges of invasion of privacy. Employees make this claim when the company checks and reads their e-mails, and uses what it finds, for disciplinary proceedings. Some companies use a software filtering application that searches e-mail content for inappropriate words pre-defined in the program and alerts management to the violators. If you want to win these cases, your policy, as an employer, should be clear on issues of privacy and ownership of your network and computer systems.

The drafting of an effective policy takes a lot of thought about your corporate culture, the kind of atmosphere you want to create among employees, and how your employees use your company's technology, especially the Internet, and your e-mail network. One policy does not fit all; each company must find its comfort level with what it will, or won't, permit as acceptable use.

I've put together a guide of twenty essential points to consider when drafting a formal policy. If you're thinking about adopting a policy to cover all aspects of employees' use of your company's e-mail system, and their access to the Internet, or if you have a policy already in place, you should check these out to be sure you've considered these issues:

Tapper's
20 POINT GUIDE
for
AN EFFECTIVE E-MAIL/INTERNET POLICY

1. Ownership. Make it clear that the company owns the e-mail system and, therefore, privacy should not be expected. The computers, software, network, and all information generated on these computers are company property. Limit the use of e-mails to business purposes only. Emphasize that all "content" created by any employee is company property. State boldly that any employee who uses the system does so, knowing the system is not private.

This is to disavow employees of any "expectation of privacy." Almost every court case tackling the issue of an invasion of privacy relies on an analysis of whether a person had a "right" to "expect" privacy in the particular situation. So far, employers are winning, where they can show an employee's expectation of privacy was entirely unfounded, in view of the employee's signed acknowledgment of the company's policy, and confirmation that she understood it. When a company bars employees from access to the e-mail and Internet system, unless they click an acknowledgment of awareness and understanding of the policy online, that evidence is very powerful in the employer's favor.

2. Right of access. This takes the privacy issue one step further, and specifically reserves a right of access to everything on the computer. Disavow any expectation of privacy when using the e-mail network, and as an employer, reserve the right to access, monitor, audit, retrieve, download, erase, and disclose any e-mail message, including the right to override and change passwords to the system. Specifically mention Internet use, and the reservation of the right to monitor all such use, including Web sites, chat rooms, newsgroups, file downloads, and all communications sent, or received, via the company's systems, and its access to the Internet.

3. Unacceptable Messages. Be clear as to what kind of messages are unacceptable. It's far better to be specific here, and not just list vague, and undefined, categories like "derogatory comments," "defamatory comments," or "inappropriate" messages. Those kinds of terms do nothing to clarify your policy to employees without giving further examples. You might say "inappropriate" includes: "messages, including cartoons, graphics, pictures, jokes, and text, that are harassing, threatening, discriminatory, sexual in nature, or offensive—as determined by the recipient or company officials who review them." Is this censorship? You bet it is! No employee has the "right" of free speech in the company's e-mail system. Some companies list certain abusive words that have no place in business e-mails, such as the ubiquitous four-letter "f- word," which not only could offend the recipient, but also a jury of average citizens when it's read, out of context, in open court. Be sure to include, under this same umbrella, any files attached to an e-mail that serve the same purpose.

Also, cover such issues as transmission of religious or political messages in the workplace, chain letters, and pyramid sales schemes. Not only do chain letters and pyramid sales schemes (where the message solicits you to forward the e-mail to a number of additional people so as not to break the chain) put you at risk of liability, but they infringe on employee productivity. If the scheme is illegal, everyone who "forwarded" the message is an accomplice, and participant in it. And once the message is forwarded, that person's name is on the electronic list, forever. Sadly, many people are not even aware of their risk of involvement here.

4. Unauthorized activities. Prohibit the sending, or receiving, of advertisements or solicitations through the system, unless specifically authorized by company officials.

5. Confidentiality. Include reminders about what information is specifically proprietary and confidential to the company, including the kind of information considered to be company trade secrets, which should not be sent to anyone via e-mail, or Internet, without official clearance from the company.

6. Use of another person's account. Strictly prohibit the use by one employee of an e-mail account of another. This is to deter the opportunity to engage in false pretense by sending e-mails to people from someone else's address.

7. Access to other sites. Describe what kind of sites are acceptable for visitation on the Internet, and decide on whether the Internet is to be used strictly for business purposes, or "primarily" for business reasons. Prohibit access to non-business related sites, such as adult-only, pornography sites, and even those that contain jokes and cartoons of all types. Add others according to your company's directives.

8. Downloading. Describe whether you will permit downloading of any files from an Internet site, and if so, of what kind or nature.

9. Broadcast messages. Only pre-authorized employees should be permitted to send messages that "broadcast" to a mass of employees throughout the company. Unless so authorized, no one should be permitted to send such messages.

10. Game playing. Unless you don't mind your employees spending a few hours a day playing solitaire, or racing a car around the Daytona 500 in vicarious enjoyment, make it clear that game playing is strictly prohibited.

11. Commercial activity. Some employees have businesses of their own on the side, and some conduct that activity through a Web site. State clearly your policy as to their conducting any business, other than your company's, during company time, and on company equipment. Include a prohibition against any illegal activity, and don't limit the illegality to any particular state's laws, but include "illegality" according to any laws to which the company may be subject, on the basis of its business nationwide, or worldwide.

12. Remote Access. Provide rules for accessing the company's network from remote locations, including home computers, laptops, and personal digital assistants. Make it clear how remote access is restricted to authorized employees only, and what your policy is concerning the transfer of company files to non-employees, and the downloading of company information to hard drives on home computers, or any other storage device. Include your position on sharing any company information with anyone who is not an employee of the company.

13. Password Protection. State your policy on sharing passwords with others, or changing a password without registering the change with the company's administrator.

14. Ownership of copyrights. State your policy so an employee knows, beforehand, what his rights are in this area, particularly with regard to material created by the employee during employment.

15. Unauthorized Representation. Because of such widespread distribution of notices and messages on the Internet, employees can make statements in chat rooms or newsgroups that make others think the employee "speaks" for the company. It's wise to remind employees they have no authority to speak for, or on behalf of, the company, and should not mislead anyone into thinking they do, based on their activity on the Internet or e-mail.

16. Violations/Enforcement. The same requirement goes here, as it did in the Document Retention Policy. In the E-mail and Internet Usage Policy, the employee controls most of the activity, so it's extremely important that your policy states clearly the consequences of violating the rules of use, how they will be enforced, which department will enforce them, and whether there will be a warning for a first offense, or termination, depending on the severity of the violation. Be specific. If the policy is vague or ambiguous, you leave your company open to selective enforcement, which opens the door to claims of discriminatory treatment by an employee. You've heard it before, but it bears repeating: enforce the policy across the board for all employees, no matter what their level.

17. Right to Change. Reserve the right to change the policy, and its restrictions, or allowances, from time to time.

18. Viruses. Although you would hope your employees have no intentions of wreaking havoc on innocent users of your system, or any system accessible through the Internet, it wouldn't hurt to include a prohibition of creating, sending, duplicating, or downloading viruses in any manner. Stating this as part of your policy gives your company added ammunition for termination, if it's violated.

19. Illegal Acts. What if one of your employees takes it upon himself to start soliciting a boycott of competing businesses, and in the process, he makes accusations that may be false about those businesses? Also, consider if an employee consults with his counterparts at one or two competitors, and they e-mail each other as to the prices they want to set for a scarce product that only your company and they produce for the marketplace? Price-fixing, boycotting, anti-trust concerns: these can happen innocently with untrained employees. It pays to mention these, and all other kinds of business communications that your company would want no employee to breach.

20. Acknowledgment Form. Your e-mail and Internet usage policies should be included as part of the Employee Manual, and they should have an acknowledgment form that requires each employee to acknowledge, by signing, a complete understanding of the rules of use, acceptance of the rules as a condition of using the equipment and network facilities of the company, and a clear awareness of the consequences of violating the rules. On the employee's computer, the acknowledgment should also show up as the first screen, prior to enabling access of the e-mail program, or Internet pathways, and require an affirmative click on the "yes" button to show awareness, and acceptance, of the rules.

The need to adopt formal policies is stronger than ever. As legislatures tackle privacy issues for the consumer, companies should expect new laws and new burdens. New lawsuits and claims are always close behind. For now, these policies will provide your company with a stronghold for your defense if they're drafted with clarity of purpose and enforced consistently in a non-discriminatory way. And last, but not least, you cannot ignore the importance of training your employees, not once, but on a continuing basis, so they cannot, reasonably, say they didn't understand the rules, the consequences of violations, or the company's commitment to making them work.

**A Summary Checklist
of
Tapper's 20 Point Guide
for
An Effective E-Mail/Internet Policy**

☐   1. **Ownership**.   Company owns the system.

☐   2. **Right of access**.   Company snooping allowed.

☐   3. **Unacceptable messages**.   No smoking guns.

☐   4. **Unauthorized activities**.   No solicitations.

☐   5. **Confidentiality**.   Watch it; protect it.

☐   6. **Use of another person's e-mail account**. No-no.

☐   7. **Access to other sites**.   Define off-limits.

☐   8. **Downloading**.   Define allowable use.

☐   9. **Broadcast messages**.   Prior approval required.

☐   10. **Game playing**.   Prohibited, period.

☐   11. **Commercial activity**.   Personal vs. business.

☐   12. **Remote access**.   Tight controls required.

☐   13. **Password protection**.   Don't be lax.

☐   14. **Ownership of copyrights**. Company owns all.

☐   15. **Unauthorized representation**. Binding agents?

☐   16. **Violations/enforcement**.   Be clear, consistent.

☐   17. **Right to change**.   Amendments expected.

☐   18. **Viruses**.   Malicious activity=termination.

☐   19. **Illegal acts**.   Zero tolerance policy.

☐   20. **Acknowledgment form**. No more "didn't know."

Epilogue

So, what do you do with all you know now?

The wisest course of action would be to find those pitfalls and traps that I've identified in your workplace, and take precautionary steps to eliminate them (if you haven't started already). You're now powerfully equipped, and far ahead of your colleagues, because I've given you enough know-how to eliminate smoking guns from your own words and actions. For the good of the company, and your own good, so you don't get trapped unwittingly by others, you'll need to spot when your colleagues are treading in dangerous territory by the things they say, do, or write.

Be a good observer. Look for the breeding grounds around you; every workplace has them. The ones we've identified should keep you busy, but there are always more.

Think defensively. When you write an e-mail, don't send it until you're satisfied with answers to these:

√   What will this sound like tomorrow? Six months from now?
√   What if my supervisor reads it? Or, the CEO or Chairman of the Board?
√   Am I proud of what I'm saying?
√   If I had a detractor out to "get" me, could what I say here boomerang, if twisted and turned in a negative way?

The next time you talk on a cell phone, or use voice-mail to leave a message, the advice I gave you should make you more circumspect in what you say. What about the papers and files you have on your desk, and in your other office areas? Now that you know the myth of confidentiality, and the importance of an attorney-client communication, you can prepare your writing, and protect the contents, with a heightened sensitivity not only to the dangers of mishandling it, but to the reality that an "outsider" may someday read it. Think of the security compromises you make before downloading your electronic files to storage disks and hard drives, printing your work at shared printer stations, or copying your reports and projects at in-house or outside copy centers.

Don't let your computer become a "virtual" warehouse of evidence for trial lawyers whose bloodhounds are waiting to sniff out its archived data. Clean out those old files and e-mails—they're only courting trouble for you and your company. Get rid of old drafts. You don't need to save the twenty versions of contract drafts, once you have the final, signed one.

You know the hot buttons that inflame a jury toward punitive damages, so re-focus your operations, particularly in product liability areas, to eliminate this danger. And when you're faced with a crisis, don't forget the Eleven Commandments for your spokesperson, and by all means, follow the Eight Rules of Crisis Management now, *before* the crisis.

Be prepared. Neither you, nor your company, need look like a deer caught in headlights when your opponents come knocking. With a good document retention policy, and an E-mail and Internet usage policy that includes the points raised by Tapper's 20-Point Guide in place, and with oversight and enforcement procedures running smoothly, you'll have a defense arsenal that should serve you well. Your company's fortress will be fortified.

It's frustrating, though, when companies pay inadequate or no attention to the practice of preventive law and pro-active risk management. The company's braintrust focuses on the "up," or revenue, side, and that means marketing, new business development, strategies for competitive advantage, sales targets, and sales quotas. At the same time, risk management is considered the "down" side, a tolerated cost-center. If a company elevates its risk management functions from the darkness of a cost-center mentality to a fresh, new light, as a revenue center—yes, I said *revenue center*—the financial rewards will, in less time than you'd think, multiply faster than your traditional revenue growers.

If you build a defense shield of proactive policies and procedures, and consistently enforce them, you'll reduce your potential for liability, and eliminate exposure to punitive damages, at a savings far greater than the cost of implementing the plan. Each claim or lawsuit "saved" from happening will unclog a financial artery, allowing gross revenue to flow freely to the bottom line, without clotting for payment of lawyers' fees, settlements, litigation costs, and judgments. That means more revenue "captured," and made available for strategic use.

What percentage of your company's gross revenue makes it to the bottom line? Many employees don't realize that for every dollar that reaches that line as net profits, or net disposable income, it took many more dollars in gross sales revenues to generate it. Just suppose you have a small lawsuit in which you've incurred $30,000. in lawyers' fees for defense. That $30,000. could have been net disposable income, and your company may have had to generate $150,000., or more, of gross sales revenues to get it— not even accounting for the amount of any judgment, settlement, or costs of trial! Multiply that by the number of lawsuits against your company, and the very real potential of jury verdicts reaching well into the millions, and see how the numbers can be staggering.

All of your team works so hard to attract those gross revenue dollars to your front door, but who's keeping an eye on how fast they're escaping through the back? If you re-focus the "down" side to make it an "up" side, with an aggressive program to "weed-out" the smoking guns that cost you so much in liability, you can achieve amazing financial rewards.

Whatever you do, don't get complacent. Don't let your guard down. The world of smoking guns isn't static. It follows the dynamics of the workplace, and many employees today are in a stressful state with uncertain economic times, shifting job functions, and a diminishing workforce that leaves the survivors doing two jobs for the price of one. Low morale affects job performance in a negative way, and that leads to laxness and poor attitude about the company—strong ingredients that can catch you tripping in the minefields of smoking guns. And, as sure as government at every level creates new laws and regulations, with loopholes seized by ambitious trial attorneys, you can bet that new opportunities for breeding grounds are always on the horizon.

You have between these covers what you need to know to protect yourself and your company. Knowledge is power. Make sure you do your part to GAIN THE ADVANTAGE BEFORE THE OTHER SIDE TAKES IT!

About the Author

Jack Tapper is a dynamic attorney with more than 30 years' experience in private practice, and as in-house corporate counsel to major Fortune 500 companies, where he supervised the defense of litigation, nationwide, and created preventive risk control programs among six national brands, with multiple subsidiaries.

After graduating with a Juris Doctorate degree from The University of Pennsylvania Law School, he practiced law in New Jersey for 19 years in a successful practice emphasizing litigation, risk management, corporate, and commercial law, while counseling clients from sole proprietors to key management in the Fortune 500.

In 1990, he transitioned from outside counsel to in-house corporate counsel, in a leading casino/hotel company in Atlantic City, New Jersey, which operated on a 24 hour/7 day basis with 4,000 employees. Shortly thereafter, the parent company recruited him for headquarters' operations in Tennessee where, as Associate General Counsel, he managed the nationwide defense of litigation for three major hotel chains, with worldwide brands, and over 1000 franchised, and owner-managed, hotel operations, including a major casino gaming chain of hotels and resorts. In addition to handling litigation, he counseled the corporate risk management divisions, and created risk control programs that were benchmarks for future development.

Out of 28,000 employees, he was selected as a finalist for The Chairman's Award, the company's highest corporate award, for Outstanding Individual Performance—the first time an in-house lawyer had won such approval.

Audiences everywhere praise him for his lively and informative presentations on how employees can reduce liability risks, and cut costs of future claims.

Mr. Tapper's presentational skills come, not only from his legal experience, but from his teaching and administrative background as well. While in private practice, he served as Director of the Legal Technology Program at Burlington County College in Pemberton, New Jersey, where he was instrumental in designing, implementing, and administering a 2-year degree program for Legal Assistants. He wrote the curriculum for numerous legal courses, and was responsible for recruiting, leading, and managing a professional teaching team for the Legal Technology Program, which received recognition by the American Bar Association for meeting its national standards.

As a Sr. Adjunct Professor, Mr. Tapper taught law courses for ten years on the subjects of Civil Litigation, Legal Skills and Methods, Partnership and Corporate Law, and Writing Skills, where he developed his passion for public speaking, and became known for his charismatic, energetic style, and "tell it like it is" approach, which made him a most-favored professor in the curriculum.

In January, 2000, he became President and CEO of Risk Control Center, Inc., a consulting firm and business training company, headquartered in Memphis, Tennessee. The company develops "in-house" educational programs and training sessions on risk management and litigation management topics for key executives, mid-level managers, and supervisors. Mr. Tapper also presents at seminars on eye-opening "What You Need To Know" topics that provide substantive information, in an entertaining way.

As an attorney, he's licensed in all courts of New Jersey and Tennessee, and is admitted to practice in the U.S. Supreme Court, the U.S. District Court for the District of New Jersey, the U.S. District Court for the Western District of Tennessee, and the Third Circuit of the U.S. Court of Appeals.

To bring Jack Tapper into your organization to speak at your next business meeting or convention, you can contact him, via the publisher, care of Simon-William Publishing, Inc. at P.O. Box 17123, Memphis, TN 38187-0123. Or,visit him on the Web, at www.jacktapper.com

Index